HARNESS YOUR
DARK SIDE

HARNESS YOUR
DARK SIDE

*Mastering Jealousy, Rage, Frustration
and Other Negative Emotions*

AL GALVES, PH.D.

New Horizon Press
Far Hills, New Jersey

Galves, Al
Harness Your Dark Side:
Mastering Jealousy, Rage, Frustration and Other Negative Emotions

Cover design: Wendy Bass
Interior design: Scribe Inc.

Library of Congress Control Number: 2011935084
ISBN-13: 978-0-88282-383-6

New Horizon Press

Manufactured in the U.S.A.

16   15   14   13   12   1   2   3   4   5

Author's Note

This book is based on the author's research, personal experiences and clients' real life experiences. In order to protect privacy, names have been changed and identifying characteristics have been altered except for contributing experts. For purposes of simplifying usage, the pronouns his/her and s/he are sometimes used interchangeably. The information contained herein is not meant to be a substitute for professional evaluation and therapy with mental health professionals.

To Nancy

Contents

Prologue

DISCOVERING YOUR DARK SIDE

In *Harness Your Dark Side* we will focus on how to build a more fulfilling, satisfying life, a fascinating task that we all face. It is my strong belief that we have come to depend too much on our rational abilities and to distrust our more basic faculties.

We will explore how to use those basic faculties—animal instincts, primordial drives, deep beliefs and "negative" emotions—to create a life that works for you and how to use those valuable parts of yourself that have been underdeveloped and neglected.

What do I mean by basic instincts, drives and emotions? I am referring to our powerful desires to survive and thrive, to eat what we want to eat, to sleep where we want to sleep, to mate with whom we want to mate, to take care of our loved ones and to construct things that will help us do that. We can learn to use these inborn drives, to use *all* of our faculties, not only the ability to think, remember and analyze but also the ability to run, jump, make music and art, build things, help one another, procreate, laugh, tumble and even the ability to feel and use emotional and physical pain.

The rational faculty—the part of ourselves that we use to think, understand, plan, create and analyze—has been, in my opinion, overvalued by our culture. Certainly, the rational faculty is useful. We can thank it for the scientific and industrial progress of the past five hundred years. But it won't help us know what is important to us, make choices about where to focus our energies or use our painful emotions to identify what we care about and do what we have to do to take care of it. In order to use our rational faculty well, we need to harness it to the yoke of our basic instincts, drives and emotions. This book will help you accomplish that most important of tasks.

The story of Phineas Gage

Phineas Gage's story is one of the great narratives of psychology. Gage was a talented foreman on a railroad crew, highly respected for his technical and supervisory ability. One day while he was setting an explosive device to remove rock from the track's path, an explosion sent a steel bar through Gage's brain. Miraculously, it didn't kill him or disable him physically. Upon his recovery, he was able to move, walk and converse in a normal way. But the accident changed his character. Previously very socially appropriate and able to make good decisions regarding his career and future life, he became a social misfit and lost his ability to work effectively. He used profanity indiscriminately and seemed not to care how he affected other people. Gage was unable to maintain his attention long enough to perform any but the most menial and mindless of jobs. He became both impulsive and stubborn and could not make effective decisions about his life. Sadly, he plunged into an existence of intermittent employment, drunkenness, random brawling, indiscriminate wandering and, eventually, early death. The injury to his brain had not affected his language ability or his abilities to move normally or experience the senses of sight, touch and hearing. But somehow it had taken away his ability to anticipate the future and plan accordingly within a complex social environment, his sense of responsibility to himself and others and his ability to orchestrate his survival deliberately. The injury to Gage became the object of medical inquiry and sparked the interest of neuroscientists studying the functioning of the brain and its impact on personality. One of those scientists was Antonio Damasio.[1]

Feeling bad: the key to using your reasoning powers

Damasio studied people who, because of brain damage, were unable to feel emotions.[2] If you met people like this you wouldn't notice anything different about them at first. They would carry on conversations, think rationally and appear quite normal. But if you got to know them and became familiar with their lives, you would learn the value of being able to feel bad. By not being able to feel bad, these people would be unable to make good choices about their lives. They would make bad business decisions but wouldn't feel bad and so wouldn't take corrective action. They would be in unsatisfying relationships but wouldn't really "know" it and wouldn't do anything about it. They would wrestle at great length over the simplest of alternatives, like where to go eat, because they couldn't "feel" their way to a satisfying decision. It turns out that the only way you can "know" you've made a bad decision is to feel it in your body. You can't know it in your head. If you can't feel bad, you can't make very good use of your rational faculty, at least not in making important life decisions. It turns out that if you can't feel, you can't think very well.

Becoming friendly with your dark side

At age twenty-five, I was a member of the staff of the Peace Corps Training Center near Arecibo, Puerto Rico. The Center was located high in the central mountains, a beautiful setting looking down on Dos Bocas Reservoir, replete with tropical foliage, little frogs that peeped through the night, dramatic thunderstorms, cool nights and beautiful, warm days. We were designing a new kind of training program for Peace Corps volunteers, an "unstructured" program in which the trainees would be encouraged to take some control over their schooling and use their experience of organizing themselves as a laboratory for learning about community development. The work was invigorating, inspiring and challenging. My fellow trainers were energetic, committed, bright and fun to be around. My wife, a wonderful woman with whom I was deeply in love, was working alongside me. Nevertheless, I became severely depressed.

No matter what time I went to sleep I woke up at 1 A.M. and was not able to fall back asleep. Every night I laid in bed for hours, tossing and turning, alternately sweating and freezing. There were times during the day when I went completely blank and was unable to function. Often, I felt as if nothing mattered, nothing made any difference, nothing had any meaning. Other times I was shaking, jittery or unable to speak clearly. Simple tasks became chores of monumental proportions, requiring every ounce of energy and concentration to keep others from observing that I was obviously in big trouble. It took great effort to keep people from realizing what was going on with me. I went to a local doctor who told me that I was suffering from a tropical disease called "la monga" and who prescribed what I thought was an antibiotic but later learned was a muscle relaxer. Sure that it was something more serious, I looked up the symptoms of brain tumors in *The Merck Manual* and was convinced that was what was going on. So I went to the Peace Corps director and told him I was quitting and going to the Mayo Clinic to take care of my brain tumor.

He committed one of those heroic acts which to him was a no-brainer but to me was a lifesaver. He told me not to quit, to keep working and he would make me an appointment with a doctor and give me whatever time I needed to be treated. The doctor he sent me to was a Puerto Rican psychiatrist who had been trained in psychoanalysis.

"There's only one rule here," the psychiatrist said. "You lie on the couch and you say everything that comes to your mind." Ready to do virtually anything he asked me to do, I thought: *Since my mind is always working, if I'm silent he'll know I'm withholding something from him.*

I did my best to comply with the instructions. I started feeling better by the third session. I went for treatment three times a week for six months and twice a week for the next year. It was the best thing I ever did for myself.

Eventually the psychiatrist helped me understand why lying on a couch saying everything that came to my mind, with him sitting behind me, out of sight and hardly doing anything, was so helpful. "When you say everything that comes into your head," he explained, "you expose the crazy part of yourself and you become more comfortable with it."

The stuff that came out of my mouth was shameful, childish, embarrassing, ugly, homicidal, stupid, ridiculous, egomaniacal, narcissistic. I hated my father, wanted to murder him. I wanted to have sex with every female. I wanted to be grander, smarter, more powerful than everyone else in the world. I was afraid of being weak, selfish, dense, aggressive, sexually impotent, unlikable and overly competitive, all of which, of course, I was.

There was something about saying all of these things in the presence of another human being that was profoundly affirming and comforting. *I could reveal all of this ugliness, selfishness and stupidity without being struck down, denigrated or punished,* I reflected. *Maybe I can live with myself after all.*

The psychiatrist didn't say very much during our meetings. Several times I told him about going out dancing with women other than my wife in local hotels and he replied in his deep baritone voice: "Man is not monogamous." My eyes widened. *What's he talking about?* He pointed out all my slips and referred back to things I had said in previous sessions. During one session I said I wanted to take him up to the roof of one of the luxury hotels in San Juan and throw him off. I now know that he was thinking to himself, *It's working.*

Coming face-to-face with these shameful, horrible, unacceptable parts of myself, becoming more comfortable with them and starting to believe I could live with them was profoundly healing. Ironically, in a way I have since come to understand, that process also enabled me to be more loving and forgiving of my father, better at working with other people, a more loving husband and father and a more cooperative member of my community.

Slowly, the depression began to lift. Gradually I became more able to focus my attention on work and to be at ease with other people, including my wife. What had happened? How had this therapy been helpful? What happened is that I became more comfortable with my dark side: the drives, deep beliefs and feelings which were inside of me but which were so "wrong," alien and horrifying. Becoming more comfortable with them and accepting of them meant I didn't have to spend so much energy keeping them hidden from myself and others. Becoming aware of those drives, feelings and deep impulses also made it possible for me to manage them, to integrate them into my personality, to get some control over them instead of having them control me. And coming to understand that those feelings and impulses were normal and understandable reactions to what I had experienced in my life made them much less shameful than they had been. I had gotten in touch with parts of myself that had been hidden and repressed. I had become whole, more able to use all of myself in the process of building my life. And, as a result of being less troubled by the emotional turmoil inside, I was more able to use my rational faculties to work effectively.

I have since learned that we all face this task of learning to acknowledge and accept the parts of ourselves that are scary, dangerous and shameful. We tackle that task in all kinds of ways at different times of our lives with varying degrees of success.

The long, hard path

This life-building task is not an easy one. By the time we are conscious enough and powerful enough to start taking control, we have been saddled with a bunch of givens which we didn't choose but which we have to manage nonetheless.

We are given a body and mind with which to work. The body and mind come with a built-in operating system, but there isn't any manual or help button that we can use to get a handle on how it works. The operating system includes some very important givens: what we need, what is important to us, what drives us, what we're scared of and what we want to avoid. In order to use those givens we need to pay attention to what happens to us and to how we feel about what happens to us so that we can react in ways that work for us.

We are also given a bunch of software in the form of beliefs, assumptions, attitudes and feelings that grow in us through our early relationship with our parents, a factor we don't have any control over but which has a great impact on us. It turns out that we can make some changes in that software, but it's not going to be easy.

There are some things about living in the United States at the beginning of the third millennium which contribute to the difficulty of the task. First, we are imbued with the myth that every American has an equal opportunity to be rich, famous, happy and wonderful. If we aren't rich, famous, happy and wonderful, we have nobody to blame but ourselves. This makes for a society in which people have very little compassion for themselves.

Second, when we feel sad, angry, jealous or afraid, because we aren't as rich, famous, happy or wonderful as we want to be or as someone else is, we are encouraged to take a pill that will mask the feelings rather than use the feelings to build a more satisfying life. The pill will deaden those feelings and help us take our minds off them. But it will also keep us from using those painful feelings to become aware of what is wrong, what needs to be addressed and changed, what we need to do to live more the way we want to live. Instead of using the operating system and software to perform the difficult task of building a life that fits our uniqueness, we go for an easy fix that may make things feel better in the short run but will keep us from building a satisfying life in the long run.

Third, if you do opt for the more difficult but more satisfying option of learning how to use *all* of yourself to live the way you want to live, you're going to have to jump through more hoops and pay more than if you just took the pills. If you want the pills, all you have to do is go to your primary care doctor. If you want help with building a life, you'll have to get a referral from your primary care doctor and spend considerable time finding somebody with whom you can do that difficult work in relative comfort. You'll also have to pay more out of pocket.

Fourth, the public institution which should help you learn how to build a life—school—will help you learn how to read and write and do basic math. It will work hard to help you learn about science, higher mathematics, history and the English language. It will go to great lengths to teach you how to obey rules and force yourself to focus on the subject matter and material it thinks is important. It will be of some use to you in learning how to relate to other human beings. But school will be virtually useless in helping you to figure out what is important to you, what you care about, what you are passionate about and how to harness that caring and passion in the process of building your life. It will also be of little use in helping you learn how to use the three faculties which are indispensable to the task of life-building: your will, your emotions and your basic drives.

Building a satisfying, fulfilling life is not an easy task. It takes time, effort and courage. But the rewards are great. You'll use all of your abilities in a way that most people don't get to. If you want to, you'll have nourishing love relationships, friends and family. If you want to, you'll make a pretty good living. You'll be relatively healthy. You'll contribute to the welfare of your fellow human beings. If you want to, you'll experience more of life than most people do. And, perhaps best of all, you'll be relatively free, autonomous and fully alive.

Chapter 1

THE MISSION:
USE YOUR WHOLE SELF

This organism that we inhabit can analyze, remember, solve, build, create, love, hurt, throw, catch, decide, hit, discover, understand, help, destroy and slide down slippery slopes on slats of wood and metal. How in the world do we learn to manage this complex piece of machinery in a way that helps us and our fellow organisms live well? That's the question that I've been trying to answer all of my life and that forms the basis of this book.

These wonderful capacities that we have can be used for good or for ill. They can be used to create or to kill, to protect or to harm. Our brains can be used to analyze, discover, understand, plan, decide and build. But they can also be used to imagine that we are right when, in fact, we are wrong; to believe that other people are angry with us when, in fact, we are angry with them; to erroneously justify bad behavior; to point the finger at others instead of owning our own imperfections; to convince ourselves that we should avoid doing what we really want to do.

We can use our anger to know what is threatening us and take action against it or to kill others and ourselves. Jealousy can tell us what we want and motivate us to go after it or it can turn us into hateful misanthropes. From sadness we can learn what is precious to us and commit ourselves to nurturing and protecting it or we can become so depressed that we hurt ourselves. Fear can keep us from hurting ourselves or it can keep us from doing what we need to do.

In the same way, our passions and drives can be helpful or harmful. Our powerful drive to eat what we want to eat, live where we want to live, love whom we want to love and express ourselves the way we want to express ourselves can be used to nurture ourselves and our families or to destroy the world and its inhabitants. Our deep, hidden beliefs and assumptions about ourselves and others can keep us going in the right direction or bring us to doom and gloom.

This book is designed to help you use the powerful, wonderful, painful and dangerous parts of yourself to live the way you want to live and to help your loved ones live the way they want to live. It is designed to give you practical approaches as well as insight, to be useful as well as interesting.

You must deal with pain and discomfort in the short run in order to achieve happiness and joy in the long run. The message is not to "feel good;" it is to "feel everything." You will learn to use the stress response to love more the way you want to love and work more the way you want to work. You will become aware of the deep, hidden beliefs and assumptions that drive your behavior so that you can control them instead of them controlling you. You will find how to "own" the parts of yourself that you don't like and wish weren't there so that you can use them instead of having them use you and learn how selfishness at the right times and in the right ways can help you contribute to the lives of those you love. You will realize how to use your body to find intimacy without losing yourself.

Here are my two basic messages:

- Everything you experience in your body and your mind is meaningful and has a reason behind it. Human beings are not random organisms. There is nothing random about us.

- The key to living well is being aware of all that you are experiencing—especially the painful and uncomfortable stuff—and using it to love the way you want to love and express yourself the way you want to express yourself.

Using the dark side's message center

To achieve the mission, you're going to have to learn to use your body; that is, notice what is going on in your body and become aware of the sensations that are occurring in your body. This is important because your body and the sensations in it are powerful and unique sources of information for you. This is a notion that has been lost in our culture, which is so focused on the mind and rationality. If you spend some time in a typical public school, you will hear teachers talk about values, morality and character. But you won't see any of them teaching children how to use their bodies to know what is valuable to them. This is unfortunate, because you can't know what is important to you, what you value and what is right for you except through experiencing sensations in your body.

Actually, when we're talking about knowing what you like and dislike, what you are attracted to and afraid of, it doesn't make sense to make a distinction between the body and the mind. That distinction is a false dichotomy. When it comes to attaching value to things, our minds and bodies are so inextricably interrelated that it is impossible to tease out which is dominant, which comes first or even how they sequence together.

If I ask you, for example, whether you like chocolate ice cream better than strawberry ice cream, you will be able to tell me without seeming to access your bodily sensations. But the way you know that is through your taste buds, part of your body.

If I ask you what is important to you, you will give me an answer that seems to come from your rational faculty, your mind. But if you think about how you really know that it is important, you will realize that you came to know it in your body, through some kind of visceral mechanism, through feeling an emotion. We can only feel emotions in our body. They are visceral processes. We feel them in our stomachs, muscles, heads or entire bodies. We feel them; then we give them names based on what we think may be causing the bodily sensation. So the feelings of fear and anger are quite similar: they include a sudden rush of energy, a queasiness in the stomach, perhaps a tightening of muscles and quickening of the breath. We only distinguish between them when we are aware of what is causing the bodily sensations.

When I use the term "body" I am referring to three different phenomena: bodily sensations (feeling tense, jittery, numb), sensory input (taste, touch, sight, hearing) and movement. All three are important in knowing what is going on with you. You may think of emotion as being something separate. But we feel emotions in the body and experience them as bodily sensations.

Sensory input—receiving information from hearing, sight, touch and taste—and movement are clear to most people. But many of us are less familiar with getting information from bodily sensations, feelings that we feel inside the body. They are sensations such as queasiness or jumpiness in the stomach, numbness in the fingers or toes, tightness around the eyes or in the chest. They include pain in all of its forms. When I am anxious or angry, I experience a tight band of pressure around my head. When I am afraid, I often feel a queasiness in my stomach. Other words that describe common bodily sensations are clammy, throbbing, nauseous, quivering, jittery, tingly, shaky and dizzy.

Here is a more comprehensive list:

twitchy	dull	sharp	achy	smooth
jagged	frozen	airy	thick	trembling
shivery	chills	vibration	itchy	locked
intense	mild	numb	flaccid	moving
congested	expanding	tight	puffy	bubbly
tingly	shaky	paralyzed	sweaty	moist
clammy	jumbly	frantic	energized	stringy
damp	electric	fluid	light	fuzzy
dense	cool	throbbing	faint	strong
pulsing	constricting	warm	radiating	shuddering
bloated	flushed	pressure	jumpy	tense
wobbly	dizzy	nauseous	spinning	suffocating
tremulous	breathless	quake	quivery	
pounding	heavy	spasming	goose bumps	

Now try an exercise that is designed to help you begin experiencing your bodily sensations so you can get more information from them.

Getting in Touch with Your Body

1. Find a comfortable place to sit. Begin to calm down by imagining that the tension in your body is dripping out through your fingers and toes. Feel the tension leaving your muscles as you sink into the floor or chair. Allow gravity to pull you into the chair or the floor. Give in to gravity; let your body feel its force.

2. As you become calmer and calmer, bring your attention to your breathing. Just notice your breathing without trying to change it. Notice the steady rhythm. Notice how your stomach expands with the in-breath and contracts with the out-breath. Notice your breath passing through your nostrils and your mouth. Just focus on your breathing.

3. As you are focused on your breathing, you will notice that thoughts come into your head. Just notice them and then let them go. Notice them and say goodbye to them and bring your attention back to your breathing.

4. Now that you are calm, quiet and focused inside, you can notice anything that is going on in your body. It might be some pain somewhere, a tightness or numbness, a slight jumpiness or feeling of energy or a slight fuzziness, clamminess or shakiness. Or you might not notice anything and that is fine also. You can just continue to focus on your breathing.

5. When you notice some sensation in your body, stay with it. Even if it is pain, go into it. Imagine that you can breathe into it. Instead of trying to avoid it, focus even more intensely on it. Get into it. Stay with it and notice what happens to it. If it moves, go with it. Follow it. If it goes away, just let it go and notice what is going on in the rest of your body. The idea is to be with yourself, to accept

what is going on in your body with no attempt to avoid it, manage it or control it. Just notice it and follow it, wherever it goes and whatever happens to it.

This exercise will give you some practice in noticing what is going on in your body. By quieting down and getting rid of some of the internal noise that we all live with, you become able to detect the subtle changes that go on inside. These are messages to you. They have valuable information for you, information about what you like and dislike, what you want and don't want, what is threatening you, what you want to get rid of, what you want to go after, what is important, what you need to be more aware of.

In order to make full use of these messages, you need to be able to connect them with thoughts. The next exercise is designed to give you some practice in doing that.

Connecting Bodily Sensations and Thoughts

1. Repeat steps one through three in the "Getting in Touch with Your Body" exercise described previously.
2. As you sit calmly and quietly focused inside your body, ask yourself one of these questions:
   - What is keeping me from feeling pretty okay?
   - What is missing from my life?
3. As you think about the answer to the question, pay attention to what comes up in your body, to any bodily sensation that you notice. Whatever you notice, stay with it. See if you can expand it or contract it. Stay with it. Focus on it. Go into it. Follow it wherever it goes or however it changes. That's it. Just stay with it. Notice it. And follow it.
4. Now ask yourself: "If this sensation had a voice, what would it tell me? What would be its message to me?"
5. Listen carefully to whatever comes up. It might be a thought, an image, a sensation or an internal voice. Whatever it is,

even if it seems silly, stupid, inconsequential or trivial, pay attention to it.

6. Now ask yourself: "What would be some next steps that would make sense for me?" Again, be open to whatever comes up in a spirit of inquiry, curiosity and exploration. Notice and accept whatever comes up—even if it doesn't seem very promising.

7. Leave the exercise and let things be.

Chapter 2

NEGATIVE EMOTIONS: THE ROAD TO AWARENESS

O ne of the key components of your dark side is the group of so-called "negative" emotions: anger, fear, anxiety, jealousy, sadness and guilt. They are part of the dark side, because they are painful and, when not used properly, can cause people to hurt themselves and others. But, like all emotions, they are the key to self-understanding and self-management. They are what have enabled us to survive as long as we have as a species. They tell us what is important to us, what we need to pay attention to, what we need to be careful about, what we like and don't like and even how we should treat other people.

Emotions

Emotions are somewhat neglected stepchildren in the psychological family. Since the Renaissance, our culture has favored reason, cognition and logic over emotion. Analytical and technical thinking has fueled the industrial, scientific, technological and digital revolutions that have occurred over the past five hundred years. In the twentieth century, psychology was ruled largely by behaviorism, which doesn't pay any attention to emotions, and by cognitive science, which focuses on information processing and sees the mind as similar to a computer.

In recent years, psychologists have come to see emotions as crucial to our well-being. We have seen how Antonio Damasio learned that if people cannot process their feelings, they can't make much use of their rational faculties. Others have come to see emotions as the key to helping people know what they want, what's important to them, what's getting in the way of what they want and what to do about it.

So what are emotions, anyway? Emotions are comprised of two components: a bodily sensation or feeling and an appraisal or interpretation of what the feeling means and what is causing it. The first sign of an emotion is some feeling in your body. It might be queasiness in your stomach, tightness around your eyes, numbness in your fingers or toes, a rush of energy in your chest or a sudden jolt of energy somewhere in your body. Chapter 1 includes a list of such feelings and an exercise you can use to get in touch with them.

That feeling is there for a reason. Something has happened, may happen or could happen that is raising a concern in you. Most likely it's a concern over something getting in the way of you loving the way you want to love, expressing yourself the way you want to express yourself or feeling okay about yourself.

In some cases—for example, when a car pulls out in front of you and you have to slam on the brakes quickly—the concern is obvious and the feeling, the interpretation and the action all happen almost instantaneously.

In other cases, you will feel the feeling but you won't immediately know what the emotion is or what it is about. You will have to pay some attention to it and spend some time figuring it out.

Some people have learned enough about their emotions so that the location of the feeling tells them what it is about. I, for example, feel fear as a queasiness in my stomach and anxiety as a tight band around my head. But for many people, the feeling is there and they are aware of it, but they don't know what the emotion is or what has brought it on. The next step for them is to spend some time figuring it out, asking such questions as:

- What is happening or might be happening that is causing me some concern?
- What do I have to do that is causing me some concern?
- What is missing from my life?
- What is keeping me from feeling okay about myself?
- What do I want badly but don't have?
- Have I lost something that is precious to me? (It may not be a person that you've lost; it may be a sense of certainty or security or some closeness with another person or anything else which you value greatly.)
- What is threatening my ability to love, work, express?
- What have I done or not done that I feel bad about?

It may take you a while to give a name to the emotion you're feeling and to become aware of what has triggered it. The same bodily feeling may be associated with different emotions. Only you can know what has brought it on, because you are the only person who is sufficiently in touch with what has been going on in your life and with what you are concerned about to be able to know. Remember, we are talking about using these emotions to build a life for yourself, not for anyone else nor for the culture or the country.

The one thing you don't want to do is ignore the feeling, decide that it is something you ate or some bug that is attacking you. My suggestion is to assume that the feeling has something to do with your life and, as a first step, ask the reflective questions of yourself.

People are reluctant to attribute uncomfortable or painful bodily sensations to emotional or psychological matters, because that means the remedy is going to be difficult and time-consuming. People believe that if the cause of these sensations is something they ate or some physical illness, they'll be able to treat it with a pill or it will eventually go away. If it is some emotional or psychological concern, they'll have to do some work on themselves or do something that is hard and scary to do. Again, I encourage you to assume that it has something to do with a concern you have about what's going on in your life and only go to the purely physical explanation after you have ruled those out.

When you are trying to figure out what the emotion is—anger, jealousy, fear, sadness, anxiety, guilt, etc.—and what event has triggered it, it helps to be aware of the context in which the emotion occurred. Nico Frijda gives an example of the importance of context:

Take the example of a person who has violated a personal standard of conduct, he says. The emotion that is induced by such an act will depend on a combination of two contextual factors: Was the action accidental or willed and are others aware of or ignorant of the violation? Accidents that others witnessed or might learn about elicit the emotion of shame; acts that could have been prevented but are not known by others evoke guilt; if others are aware of the deliberate act, the emotion will be a blend of guilt and shame.

The context can also include cultural norms. Frijda notes, for example, that personal achievement will be a source of joy for American students but not for Japanese students.[1]

Keep in mind that the event that triggered the emotion may not be an external event. It may be internal—something that you are thinking or feeling inside of you. For example, at age thirty-three a typical male is feeling pretty good about things. He likes his job, feels he is progressing well on his career path and that things are going well with his marriage and his family. Five years later he may not be feeling as good. He is in the same job and things are pretty much the same with his marriage and family. But he feels depressed. It doesn't appear that anything has changed. What is going on? Now the man is thirty-eight and thirty-eight-year-old men know they are going to die in a way that thirty-three-year-old men don't. At some point between the ages of thirty-seven and forty, the typical man becomes aware of impending death in a way that leads him to get serious about the rest of his life and to know that he really has a limited time left on the Earth. Even though nothing has changed in his external life, his internal life has experienced a profound change. If he has deep concerns about being able to do what he wants to do before he dies, he can become seriously depressed.

Again, keep in mind that the word "event" can include internal, psychological events as well as external, real-world events.

Once you have figured out what emotion you are experiencing and what has triggered it, the next step is to decide if you are going to take action or not. In the case of a car pulling out in front of you or some other immediate threat to your life, the action happens automatically. In other cases you have time to decide if you are going to take action.

In most cases, a strong emotion will get you ready to take action. But you may decide not to take action, because it will require you to do something you are not able to do, because no action appears to be feasible or because there is a high probability that taking action will cause retaliation, untimely distraction, loss of friends, etc.

There are various ways in which this process of learning from your emotions can be blocked. Some people are not very good at feeling their bodily sensations. People who have been hurt badly or suffered a lot of pain have learned to shut off the messages from their bodies. Such people may have to get some help in receiving bodily messages. The best organization I know for that is the Sensorimotor Psychotherapy Institute in Boulder, Colorado.

There also are people who are shut off from their emotions. They may feel the feeling in their bodies but not be able to connect it to an emotion. They may have learned in their early experience to ignore emotions or that emotions are not to be trusted and will only hurt them.

All of us are subject to the danger of not allowing ourselves to know what the emotion is telling us, because knowing it would make us uncomfortable or put pressure on us to do something that would be difficult and dangerous. I remember the question that was so prominently displayed at a personal growth program I attended: "What am I pretending not to know?" Given these obstacles, I encourage you to take this process of emotional awareness seriously, work at it and use it to build a life that is good for you.

"Negative" emotions get a bad rap

Many of us have been taught that emotions, especially the so-called "negative" ones, are not to be trusted, are dangerous and have little value. Parents and other authorities have told us that we should be "cool under pressure," not be "hotheaded," act "professionally," think "positively" and not be "grumpy." Nobody has taught us the value of anger, fear, sadness and jealousy.

Then again, some emotions are painful. Why would you want to feel pain? In recent years, our culture has embraced the notion that pain should be avoided at all cost, even at the cost of knowing what is important, what you like and dislike, what is threatening you, what you want to approach and what you want to avoid.

What makes me so sure that all of the emotions, even the "negative" ones, are crucial to our being able to live well? Human beings have been evolving over more than thirty million years. If any of these emotions were not useful, they would have been discarded by natural selection a long time ago. And when I think about how fine-tuned, intricate and responsive our emotional faculty is, it is clear that it has something very important to offer us.

"Negative" emotions and what's important

We have often received instructions from parents, teachers, priests and pastors, bosses, doctors, writers, even from psychologists that anger, jealousy, sadness, hatred, guilt and fear are bad, that we have to get rid of them, wipe them out of our systems.

Where has the bad rap come from? Perhaps it is because the feelings are painful and uncomfortable. Or because behavior resulting from them is sometimes dangerous, distasteful and ugly. These are certainly good reasons for emotions to have a bad rap. And there is evidence that negative feelings can be associated with illness. Numerous studies have found that depressed people suffer from impaired immune system functioning and are more vulnerable to disease than non-depressed people. Other studies have found an association between anxiety and heart disease. But there are also studies that have found a powerful connection between negative emotions and health benefits. Social psychologist and professor James Pennebaker assigned writing tasks to two equal groups of college students. One group was assigned to write about unemotional topics—their plans for the future, what they did last summer, world peace, the environment. The other was assigned to write about the most emotionally painful experiences of their lives. Members of the latter group who were disclosing intimate and painful details of their lives exhibited better immune system function and made fewer visits to the health clinic than the first group.[2]

In a study by Nicholas Hall and Denis Calandra, the immune system functioning of method actors was measured while they experienced and expressed various emotions and while they were not emoting. The researchers found that the actors' immune system functioning was strongest while they were experiencing and expressing emotions. And it didn't make any difference whether the emotion they were expressing was positive (joy or love) or "negative" (anger or jealousy).[3]

In another study, researchers divided medical students into several groups based on their personalities and followed them as they matured. They found that the group which kept a tight hold on their emotions, presenting a bland exterior to the world, was *sixteen times* more likely to get cancer than the group which freely revealed and expressed their emotions.[4]

In a study I conducted, participants in a psychological wellness workshop reported higher levels of anxiety, sadness and anger *as well as* better health than the members of a control group.[5]

How can we reconcile these conflicting findings? Are "negative" emotions helpful or harmful? The answer is that it depends on how we experience and use the "negative" emotions. If we acknowledge them, sit with them and allow them to work in us, we can learn from them, gain valuable insights and use that learning and the energy in them to address issues, solve problems and find ways to live more the way we want to live. If we push them down and try to repress them, the energy in them stays inside and makes us sick. If we run away from them or try to make believe they're not there, we fail to learn the lessons they have to offer. If we beat ourselves up because we're experiencing them, we hurt ourselves. If we let "negative" emotions explode and use them to hurt other people, we become alienated and cut off.

Earlier in my life, I played in tennis tournaments. On numerous occasions I was playing well until my mother, father or wife showed up to watch me, at which point I started playing badly and lost the match. I realized that when this happened I was saying to myself: *Oh, jeez, there's my wife (or mother or father). Now I'm in trouble. Why am I so stupid? Why do I get nervous when s/he shows up? I can't believe what a jerk I am, to get nervous like this.* And, sure enough, I started dumping balls into the net, overhitting, double faulting, etc. At some point I learned to change what I said to myself. I started saying, *Oh, there's my father (or mother or wife). I'm getting nervous. Well, it's pretty normal to get nervous when your father shows up. I certainly can't blame myself for that. I'll just keep on playing, nervousness and all. Maybe I can use the energy from that nervousness to pick up the ball quicker, get to it quicker.* As you might guess, this reaction was a lot more effective than the first.

My lesson from that experience was that it wasn't the nervousness that caused my problem; rather, it was my *attitude* toward the nervousness, getting angry at myself because I was nervous. When I learned to accept my nervousness and see it as a perfectly normal response, it became much less harmful to me. The feelings themselves are not harmful or dangerous; what may make them harmful or dangerous is how we relate to them, how we experience them and how we use them.

This makes sense to me. The human organism has been evolving over millions of years. Anything which has survived must be useful, must have survival value. This means that all of the emotions that we can experience must be valuable. If they weren't valuable, they would have been lost to us a long time ago.

If I could give one gift to my clients, it would be the ability to feel bad, to experience and use painful emotions. For clients to allow themselves to feel bad, to let the bad feelings in and let them work inside, to sit with them, to ask themselves, *Why is this feeling here? What is it trying to tell me? What can I learn from it? How can I use it to get in touch with what's bothering me, deal with it and make my life better?* To just feel bad without drinking or drugging, buying a new car, turning on the television, CD player or DVD player or taking refuge in bed—for sex or for sleep.

Jane came in to see me because she wasn't feeling anything. She didn't feel bad and she didn't feel good. She was feeling nothing. She had shut down. As we began to work, she reflected on her past. She had grown up with parents who had lots of conflict and used her as a weapon against each other. But she couldn't be upset about that. She had to be a nice little girl and not cause any problems or make things worse in the house. Eventually, her parents divorced. She, like all children, believed that somehow she had some control over her parents. Children want to believe that, because to believe they don't have any control over these people who are so important to their well-being would be too scary. She felt guilty about not being able to keep her parents from splitting up. She also had an understandable anger toward them, because they were using her against each other. But she wasn't allowed to express that anger.

Jane also had been sexually molested by her brother but, again, being a nice, compliant little girl, didn't do anything about it. In our therapy sessions, I helped her to reduce the noise level inside, to focus on what was going on in her body. As we worked, her sadness and anger came out in the form of lots of crying, sighing and fist-clenching. Slowly, she learned that her anger was justifiable, that she had no control over her parents and that it was unfair for them to use her in the way they did and to discount her feelings.

Paradoxically, as Jane became more comfortable with her anger and resentment, she also developed more compassion for her parents and the trials they went through. And she began to experience her feelings, both good and bad. As that happened, she became more aware of the difficulties in her own marriage and of her desire to become a better parent to her two daughters. She stayed in her marriage, but she opened up to her husband about her grievances and desires and became more understanding and forthcoming with her daughters. She began to build a new life for herself without leaving her marriage. Most important, she regained her ability to feel pleasure and joy as well as anger and sadness.

Learning to become more compassionate with yourself and less afraid of the feelings that are inside is a major step toward a more satisfying life. When the ice begins to thaw and break up and the water begins to flow, sometimes it flows gently and sometimes it's a raging torrent, but it flows; it moves along. You will begin to have more faith in yourself and your ability to use your feelings to deal with the dilemmas of real life.

How are these "negative" emotions useful and what do we have to do to use them well? Let's explore a handful: anger, fear, anxiety, jealousy, sadness and guilt.

Chapter 3

ANGER

A nger is extremely useful. It tells us what we don't like, what is threatening us, what we want to eliminate or what we want to be careful about. It gives us the energy we need to address things we don't like and want to get rid of or protect ourselves against. But how we use it makes a big difference. O.J. Simpson used his anger in a way that ruined his life. Martin Luther King used his anger to fuel the leadership of a non-violent civil rights movement that essentially wiped out blatant, legally protected racial segregation in this country. It may sound easy: You just have to use your anger in a smart and benevolent way. But, of course, it isn't easy at all. It's very difficult and complicated.

One of the things that makes it difficult is that when we are in the grip of the first rush of anger, when we're in the "throes" of it, we can't think very well. We can't use our rational faculty. Somehow, Martin Luther King was able to step back from the emotional rush of the anger, to get enough distance from that burst of adrenaline so that he could put his rational faculty to work in building an effective movement for social change. O.J. Simpson was apparently unable to engage his rational faculty. It appears that he threw away a life that was the envy of a nation of men. How can we understand and use this difference?

One way is to recognize that, in many cases, anger sits on top of three other emotions: shame, hurt and fear. If we can stop long enough to ask ourselves, "What is underneath this anger?" and get in touch with the shame, hurt and fear, we may be able to gain the space we need to engage our rational faculty and make a good decision about what to do with the anger.

When it is bottled up and not expressed, anger is a killer. It can make people sick and it can make them crazy. This is because there is a lot of energy in anger. If that energy isn't expressed, it burrows inside and wreaks havoc. I have treated numerous clients who suffer from fibromyalgia. Fibromyalgia is the latest diagnosis that is given to people who are troubled by constant pain and weakness but whose laboratory reports and x-rays come up negative. All of these clients have trouble expressing anger. They are nice people, reasonable and understanding. They don't want to rock the boat or cause problems. They don't want other people to see them as troublemakers or ingrates. They don't know how to be mean and assertive. They aren't comfortable being clear about what they want and going after it with a vengeance. They haven't learned how to use their anger.

Interestingly, many of these clients had trouble with their mothers. Here are three brief profiles:

Roberta's mother was an alcoholic. Like most children of alcoholics, Roberta had to take care of her mother. At the age of ten, she became a caregiver for her mother, having to take responsibility for both herself and her mother and having to spend lots of energy covering it all up. As she entered her early twenties, her relationship with her mother began to change. They became closer and more friendly and supportive of each other. Just as they were beginning to heal some of their wounds, her mother committed suicide.

Isabel came to me, because she had a history of sabotaging herself. Repeatedly, she took a job or began studying and performing so well that she was a star. Then, all of a sudden and inexplicably, she stopped going to class, got into trouble with coworkers, made unexplainable mistakes, quit or got fired. She grew up in a household in which her father absolutely doted on her. She was the "apple of his eye." He paid much attention to her and helped her grow into a very talented young woman. At the same time, he neglected her mother. Resentful and angry and either unable or unwilling to confront her husband, she took it out on her daughter, constantly criticizing, nagging, berating. No matter how hard Isabel tried, there was nothing she could do to please her mother. And she had learned that, whenever she performed well and thereby won her father's love, she would lose her mother's love. Whenever she won, she lost.

Margie's mother was a businesswoman, a firm taskmaster. Margie could never do anything well enough to satisfy her mother. Often her mother asked her to clean the living room, checked it, said, "Oh, this will never do" and asked Margie's older sister to finish the chore. One evening at the dinner table, Margie mildly suggested that her mother might not have worked very hard that day, a transgression that earned her a beating from her father and icy disdain from her mother. In her forties Margie was still obsessed with pleasing her mother.

None of these women had learned to express anger toward their mothers and all were suffering from it. After all, it's not easy to be angry with our parents. They have given us the gift of life and sacrificed on our behalf. Somewhere deep inside, we know they have done the best they could, have had to deal with their own demons and live their own lives. In many cases, they have let us know that it's not okay to be angry with them. The great psychoanalyst Alice Miller realized after working for years as a therapist that there was a simple formula for making people mentally ill: not let them be who they are and, when they get angry about it, not let them be angry.[1] That's a good description of what goes on in many households today and of how some public schools treat their students. Here's the dilemma: We need to acknowledge our anger toward our parents and find ways of expressing it even though we know they aren't to blame, they didn't want to hurt us and they were being driven by their own relentless, demanding needs. Here are three options for dealing with this dilemma:

- Find a psychotherapist who understands the importance of this process and will help you go through it.

- Write about your anger toward your parents. Don't edit what you write. Just write it in a kind of automatic writing in which you are letting the words flow out of your mind.
- Use the Chair Technique described in chapter 13 to verbally express your anger toward your parents.

One of the benefits of doing this work is that after you express your anger toward your parents, you'll find it much easier to forgive them and love them for what they have given you. But the greatest benefit is that you will find ways of using the energy in your anger to create, build, develop and contribute to other people instead of leaving the energy trapped inside, sapping your vitality and making you sick.

Anger can also be useful in helping us become more considerate of other people. When I get angry at someone else's behavior, it tells me what makes other people angry, an insight I can use to be more considerate of others. For example, I become angry when other drivers pull in front of me, making me stop or slow down. This has taught me to be more careful about pulling out in front of other drivers.

The most useful thing about anger is that it tells us what we don't like, don't want and want to eliminate. It tells us what is threatening us. And it gives us the energy we need to do something about it. This is very valuable information. If we know what is getting in the way of us loving the way we want to love and expressing ourselves the way we want to express ourselves, perhaps we can do something about it.

The one thing you don't want to do is suppress your anger, stuff it or tell yourself you shouldn't be angry or that you don't have a right to be angry. There are two reasons for this: you won't learn what you can learn from the anger and you won't use the energy in the anger, which can make you sick or depressed.

There's research evidence showing that suppressing anger is associated with increased pain, pain behavior, depression and poor adjustment to childhood sexual abuse. Being able to express anger is associated with improved performance of tasks, reduced pain and better adjustment to childhood sexual abuse.

The next exercise will help you use anger to live more the way you want to live. The exercise assumes that you have been able to separate yourself somewhat from the event that caused the anger. Oftentimes that is not the case. If you are braking to avoid a collision or reacting to a dog attack, the feeling, the figuring out and the action will occur immediately and concurrently. If you have been shamed, hurt or threatened by the behavior of another person, you may be able to step back, take a deep breath and count to ten before you react. Other times, you will become aware of some pain, numbness, tightness, tension or other bodily feeling that is there but you don't know what is causing it. Sometimes it is something you are angry about but that you don't want to acknowledge or have to deal with. In such cases this exercise can be very helpful.

Anger Exercise

Find a quiet place to sit and reflect or find a tranquil place to walk and ask yourself these questions:

- If this is anger, what is it about?
- What is threatening me, scaring me or getting in my way?
- What do I want to rid myself of?
- What, if anything, do I want to do about it?
- How will I use the energy in this anger to take care of myself?

Chapter 4

FEAR

Fear is perhaps the most useful of the "negative" emotions. Fear tells you what you need to be careful about, what can harm you, what is dangerous and what you need to avoid. It gives you the energy you need to be able to protect yourself and do what you need to do. But fear can also be hurtful to you. It can make you avoid doing what you need to do. It can keep you from addressing problems that you need to address. In extreme amounts, it can keep you from leaving the house, interacting with other people and fulfilling your responsibilities.

Fear is the trickiest of all emotions and the most difficult one to manage, because sometimes it must be quickly identified and followed with no time for reflection; other times it must be noticed and considered to see how we should respond to it.

One way of understanding this difference is to draw a distinction between rational fear and irrational fear. The one enables us to stay alive; the other keeps us from living the way we want to live, keeps us from being aware of what is going on inside us and outside us. The hard part is knowing the difference. How does one know the difference between rational and irrational fear?

One way of getting some help with this problem is checking with another person, someone you trust and who knows you well. Tell the person about your fear and see what his or her reaction is. I received that kind of help from my therapist. At the age of forty-four I was trying to figure out what to do with my life. I had gained a master's degree in public administration, spent a decade managing city, urban and regional planning activities and precipitously quit a management job at which I had been quite successful. I got scared and quickly took a similar job but was reorganized out of that position, spent three years nominally as an external consultant but really focused on singing, dancing and acting and then decided that I was going to become an organization development consultant. I knew that pursuing that goal would take me away from the city my wife loved and didn't want to leave.

In a therapy session I reported two dreams. In one, I slapped an elegantly dressed woman who had just emerged from a limousine at the corner of Fifth Avenue and 59th Street in Manhattan; slapped her so hard that it spun her around. She put her head down and walked away without saying a word or uttering a sound. In the other, the vision that appeared was of my wife's face being hit so hard by a hoe handle that it was distorted as if being seen in one of those mirrors you find at a fun house. My therapist's response was, "Those are good ways of scaring yourself." I took it to mean that I was scaring myself unnecessarily, that I was in danger of stopping myself from doing something that I wanted to do. In the years that followed, my wife and I found a way of protecting our relationship without requiring her to leave her beloved city or me to abandon my pursuit of organization development consulting.

Some people refer to this process as "walking with fear," a useful and comforting metaphor. It's not that you push fear away, beat it off or run away from it. Rather, you say "Hello" to it and bring it along with you as you do what you have set out to do.

Another way of knowing the difference between rational and irrational fear is to ask yourself: *Is this fear that I feel related in any way to the ways in which I block myself, get in my own way?* One of the keys to psychological health is knowing how you get in your own way, especially how you use thoughts and feelings to stop yourself from doing what you want to do.

There are times when it makes sense to walk with your fear and not let it stop you, to bring it along with you and let the energy in it help you do what you need to do. But what about times when you shouldn't walk with it, when you should pay attention to it and let it stop you? There is a story about Edgar Cayce, the famous psychic, who was waiting for an elevator. The elevator doors opened, he looked into it and then stepped back without getting in. The elevator then plunged to the ground floor, killing everyone in it. Somebody asked him why he hadn't gotten into the elevator. "Those people had no aura," he replied. In that case, it was a good thing that Mr. Cayce didn't walk with his fear.

Fear is perhaps the easiest emotion of which to be aware. The feelings are powerful and simple to detect. But it's not always easy to be clear about what we're afraid of. Take the cases of fear of failure and fear of success. Fear of failure may be easy to understand. But many successful people have said they learned more from their failures than from their successes. That means there are times when we should go ahead even when we are afraid of failing. Since we can never be sure that we won't fail, listening to the fear of failure would keep us immobilized.

As for fear of success, there are some good bases for that fear:

- If I'm successful, people are going to have higher expectations of me and there will be more pressure on me to perform.
- Once I'm successful, people will start taking shots at me, accuse me of not playing fair or of being a "brown-noser", etc. Once I'm successful some people will start trying to bring me down. I'll become a target.
- The more successful and lofty I become, the greater the pain of falling from grace.

The problem is that in a society which puts as much emphasis on success as ours does, it may be hard for people to accept the fact that fear of success is holding them back. It's certainly something to keep in mind.

A friend of mine who works with people diagnosed with schizophrenia tells me that one of the challenges she deals with is the fear people have of getting well. That is very understandable to me. If you get well, there is going to be pressure to perform. Expectations are going to rise. Increases in stress and anxiety are going to ensue.

Among famous performers who apparently sabotaged themselves (or worse) when they appeared to be at the top of their games, Kurt Cobain, Charlie Sheen and Amy Winehouse come to mind. The full reasons why these people fell from their perches at the pinnacle of success may never be known. However, the pressure of success, the pressure to stay on top, the impossibility of always performing extraordinarily and the difficulty of living with the knowledge of what will happen if you fail obviously placed enormous stress on them. They were apparently unable to deal with it.

To me one of the saddest stories in sports is that of Steve Howe. At age twenty-two, Howe was baseball's Rookie of the Year in the National League. A relief pitcher for the Los Angeles Dodgers, he saved the final game of the 1981 World Series and was named an All-Star in 1982. But he spent some of the best years of his athletic life out of baseball. He was suspended seven times for cocaine and alcohol abuse. He didn't pitch at all in 1984 and 1986 nor from 1988 through 1990. In 1992 he was banned for life for substance abuse, but he appealed the ruling and was reinstated. Pitching for the New York Yankees, he had one last standout season in 1994 as a thirty-six-year-old closer. But he could not repeat that success and he was released by the Yankees in 1996, ending his baseball career in 1997 in the minor leagues.

There may have been many reasons for Steve Howe's addictions. Certainly, when you are a great closer, your teammates are depending on you. And statistically, every third or fourth time you come in to close a game, you are going to fail. You are going to let your teammates down. No matter how good you are, if you can't live with that, you won't be able to go out and perform. And the more successful you are, the more pressure there is to produce consistently and save the day.

Fear Exercise

When you are aware of being afraid, find a quiet place in which to sit or a remote place to walk and ask yourself these questions:

- What is it exactly that I am afraid of?
- What is the worst thing that can happen if I walk with this fear?
- What are some reasons I might let this fear keep me from doing what I want to do?

Chapter 5

ANXIETY

More than any other emotion, anxiety is helpful in the right amounts and harmful in the wrong amounts. More precisely, research demonstrates that *moderate* anxiety helps people perform well. When it is excessive, it is harmful, painful and enervating. It may come as a surprise that very low amounts of anxiety are associated with poor performance. In a way, this makes sense. If we don't care or "shut down," it's not likely that we'll perform well.

Anxiety helps us in ways similar to fear. It tells us that we need to do something that is hard and, perhaps, scary and it gives us the energy and the sharpness to do it. It is a signal that something is wrong or that something important needs to be done. The problem with anxiety is that when that "something" is very difficult to deal with, virtually impossible to address and very scary, we don't even want to know what it is. When that happens, anxiety turns into panic and becomes extremely debilitating.

Among the most difficult patients to treat in primary care clinics are those who come in with symptoms of chest pain, shortness of breath, tingling in the arms and feet, rapid heartbeat and feeling that they are going to faint or lose consciousness. These are symptoms of heart attack and stroke and need to be taken seriously. In such cases, doctors are careful to check for signs of heart issues. Oftentimes, the laboratory tests and electrocardiograms turn up negative and, after further investigation, patients are diagnosed with panic disorder. One research study found that the typical panic disorder patient was seen by nine specialists before receiving and accepting the diagnosis.[1]

Panic attacks are very harmful. Besides being extremely scary, they cause people to lose jobs, social lives, families, health and, in some cases, their lives. Panic attacks are caused by anxiety over issues and situations that are so difficult and intractable that the sufferer doesn't even want to know what the cause is.

Moira came to my office because of panic symptoms and was accompanied by her husband, who seemed quite supportive and understanding. I asked her if there was anything going on that might make her anxious. "No," she replied, "I can't think of anything." After several minutes of conversation, she said, "My son is in the Army Reserves. He's going to be doing a tour of duty in Iraq." As soon as she said that, she broke down and cried for quite a while. Her son's deployment was scheduled to begin in two weeks. He was going to be in harm's way. Apparently in an effort to bear up, not to be a burden, not to upset those around her, Moira had pushed her fear and concern down so far that others couldn't see it and perhaps she herself wasn't consciously acknowledging it. But the body knows. The body is smarter in many ways than the mind. The mind can try to do its tricks and make believe. But the body isn't fooled by that kind of dissembling. The body reacts to some level of knowing that is deeper and more essential than that. When the body reacts and becomes activated and the person doesn't acknowledge it and find a way of using the energy from that activation, panic symptoms appear.

Once Moira calmed down and got in touch with how upset she was about her son going to war, I spent some time talking with her and her husband about how she could manage her fear and how her family members could support her.

Where did this woman learn that she shouldn't acknowledge or show her anxiety about her son being sent to war? Perhaps she learned as a child not to show her fear. Perhaps she learned from a society that encourages people to be heroic and more than human in the face of adversity. Or could it be a primordial reaction to the fear that other humans might interpret her anxiety as weakness and take advantage of her? It's hard to know. What we do know is that many people suffer greatly from panic disorder, which is caused by unacknowledged and unexpressed anxiety.

I have suffered from panic attacks numerous times in my life without consciously knowing what was causing them. Now, looking back, I do.

My first experience with panic came upon me as I was sitting in a college classroom in the presence of a very attractive coed. I suffered an attack, the worst symptom of which was an inability to swallow. I barely avoided fainting. I had no idea what was going on or what was behind it. Now, looking back, I know exactly what it was about. I wanted very much to get closer to women in every way. I had no idea about how to do that and I wasn't about to ask for any help. That is the kind of intractable predicament that causes anxiety and can result in a panic attack.

I had another bout of panic attacks at age thirty-five. I was working then as an executive in southern New Mexico. It was a great job for me—challenging, wide-ranging, complete with a manageable amount of autonomy, responsibility, visibility and power. But in order to keep it I had to do some things I didn't believe in, things I didn't think were right. Whenever I was driving to a meeting of the board of directors, I suffered a panic attack, often having to pull off the road and get out of my car until it passed. Again, I didn't know what was causing the anxiety. Now I do. I was happily married, had two children and a job I loved and that suited me well but that required me to do things that violated my moral code—the kind of dilemma that can cause a panic attack.

Panic attacks are very difficult for a psychotherapist to deal with. By definition, they appear to "come out of the blue" and to not be associated with anything that would logically cause anxiety. I help clients learn how to manage the attacks through self-talk, breathing exercises and learning how to focus on something outside of themselves or on their body sensations rather than their thoughts. I believe that is the best way to manage panic attacks. Although they are very uncomfortable, they typically last for a couple of minutes at most and are not nearly as dangerous as they seem. I also encourage clients to do some self-exploration aimed at uncovering any dilemmas they are facing that seem absolutely irresolvable and for which there are no good answers— problems so difficult they don't even want to be aware of them. In many cases, even with that encouragement, clients are unable to identify the causes of their panic attacks and are faced with having to learn to live with them or use addictive prescription drugs to dampen them.

The most important point is that anxiety is a message that there is something threatening you or there is something that you have to do that is going to be very difficult and scary. If you try not to pay attention to it or to numb it with drugs, you won't address the threat or do what you have to do. If you do pay attention to it, it will help you know what it is that is threatening you or what it is you have to do and it will give you the energy you need to do it. More than any other emotion, anxiety can help you if you use it and hurt you if you don't.

Research tells us that moderate levels of anxiety are associated with good performance. Studies of students taking the Scholastic Aptitude Test have found that students going into the test with moderate anxiety do better than students with extreme anxiety or with no anxiety.[2]

One of the best things you can do to lead a healthy, satisfying and productive life is to learn how to use anxiety. Let's take a closer look at what causes it and how to use it.

Anxiety is a response to threat and danger or to the realization that one is going to have to do something that is difficult and frightening. It might be a relatively immediate and short-term threat such as taking an exam that is very important to one's future or having to deal with a fellow employee who is causing problems. Or it might be a more fundamental and long-term threat, such as extended unemployment that leads one to doubt one's abilities or a marriage that is in jeopardy. Concerns about important relationships are especially likely to bring on anxiety.

This means that all of us, at one time or another, are going to have to deal with anxiety. Psychologist Rollo May describes it as arising from "our human awareness of the fact that each of us is a *being confronted with nonbeing.* Nonbeing is that which would destroy being, such as death, severe illness, interpersonal hostility, too sudden change which destroys our psychological rootedness."[3]

Fortunately, anxiety also gives us energy and sharpness that we can use to deal with the threat or the danger. There are three steps for facing whatever is causing the anxiety and dealing with it. The first step is to become consciously aware of what is causing the anxiety and what is being endangered. In fact, as soon as you become consciously aware of that, some of the symptoms will subside. The second step is to become clear about what you want, how the threat is causing danger to that and what you are going to do about it. The third step is to follow through and do what you have to do to address the threat or danger. Another, simpler way of saying it is that you are going to use the energy and sharpness in the anxiety to become clear about what you have to do and then do it.

What you *don't* want to do is attempt to avoid the anxiety by talking yourself out of it with self-talk statements like "Oh, I can live with this situation; it's not so bad" or "I don't like what is going on in my marriage, but it's not as bad as _____" or "I can't do anything about it because it will make it worse" or by self-medicating with drugs or alcohol or engaging in other kinds of compulsive behaviors.

Attempts to avoid anxiety lead to what Rollo May calls a "shrinking up of one's world or an impoverishment of one's personality and the surrender of autonomy." Learning how to deal with it and use it is a key to self-realization. Expression and creative use of one's capacities can occur only as one confronts and moves through anxiety-creating experiences, May explains. Danish philosopher Søren Kierkegaard is even more emphatic: "He, therefore, who has learned rightly to be anxious has learned the most important thing."[4]

You also don't want to take anti-anxiety drugs unless you cannot control the attacks on your own and your physician believes they are indicated. Those drugs will keep you from being able to use your anxiety and can turn you into an addict.

Anxiety Exercise

When you feel anxiety in your body, find a quiet place in which to sit or a peaceful path on which to walk and ask yourself these questions:

- What is creating danger to my sense of feeling okay about myself, being able to live the way I want to live and having good, positive relationships with others?
- What do I want for myself right now?
- How can I use the energy and sharpness in this anxiety to do something about it?

Take some action. Do it.

Chapter 6

JEALOUSY

Jealousy tells us what we want and don't have as well as what we are missing; certainly a useful piece of self-awareness. Knowing what we want is crucial to being able to live well. But we've been taught that it's not quite right to want. It's okay to need but not okay to want. There's something about knowing what we want and going after it with zeal and ferocity that is too self-absorbed, too selfish. Perhaps this is because jealousy has fueled dangerous and harmful behavior. But again, it's important to separate the feeling from the behavior. The feeling is potentially valuable; the behavior may not be.

I have been jealous of people who perform in musical theatre, of writers who are honored for their writing and of people who are praised for their contributions to their organizations. That jealousy has fueled my desire and my effort to perform in musical theatre, to write and to contribute to organizations I care about.

The worst kind of jealousy is the jealousy that is not acknowledged, not understood, not used. Jacob, a professor, talked to his class about this scenario: A forty-year-old mother has been married for around twenty years and has a fifteen-year-old daughter. It's likely that the sexual life of the mother has evened off into a pleasant but not particularly fiery occasional romp in the sack with her husband; for some such women, sex has become even less present than that. On the other hand, there's the fifteen-year-old daughter who is just entering into the first stirring of sexual energy and who is looking forward to the exciting blossoming of early sexuality. Only the most heroic of us would be able to avoid at least a slight tinge of jealousy in such a situation. Could it be possible that jealousy as much as anything else fuels the mother's admonishments to "Make sure you get home by a decent hour," "I don't think you should go out with him," "Take care of yourself" and "Don't do anything stupid"?

Perhaps more than any other emotion, jealousy becomes toxic when it goes underground, is repressed and stays unacknowledged. It's a difficult emotion to experience and accept. It is uncomfortable. It's a sign of weakness and it's against one of the Ten Commandments. It is the antecedent of murder and mayhem. No wonder it is maligned, degraded and given a bad rap. Still, it is valuable; we need to reclaim it and use it as a signal telling us what is missing from our lives and what we want.

There are enormous dangers in repression. Sigmund Freud was the first psychologist to discover the harm in repression. He learned from observing many people that when powerful emotions like jealousy and anger are repressed, they don't go away. Rather, they are expressed in harmful, bizarre and perverse ways. When kept inside, they make people ill. When they leak out like steam in a pressure cooker, they do so in the form of nasty attitudes and hurtful and often self-defeating behavior. Had my father been able to acknowledge and openly express his jealousy, our relationship would have been a lot better and we both would have been happier men.

One of the valuable functions of jealousy is to keep love relationships intact. As we have seen, human beings are not set up biologically to mate with only one person. But there are some important advantages to long-term, committed love relationships: bringing up children and avoiding the murder and mayhem that can result from unbridled sexual rivalry. Researchers have come to see jealousy as a powerful force that keeps romantic couples from straying and breaking up. Psychologist and professor Ayala Pines writes that the main purpose of jealousy is safeguarding love: "…jealousy aims to protect romantic relationships. It is not a useless flight of irrationality but a useful signal people can learn to interpret correctly...Jealousy makes people examine their relationships...It teaches couples not to take each other for granted...ensures that they continue to value each other and...indicates that people value the love relationship it protects."[1]

Psychology professor David Buss finds that jealousy "motivates us to ward off rivals with verbal threats and cold primate stares. It drives us to keep partners from straying with tactics such as escalating vigilance or showering a partner with affection. And it communicates commitment to a partner who may be wavering, serving an important purpose in the maintenance of love."[2]

Many of us have experienced the jealousy that arises when our partner becomes interested in someone else, begins to distance from us in various ways and we realize that our relationship is in jeopardy. It turns out that men and women are different in some important ways. Men tend to be most concerned about sexual infidelity. Women are usually more concerned about emotional connection between their mates and rivals. Some men respond to the pangs of jealousy by deploying their resources—buying flowers and jewelry for their mates, taking them out to expensive restaurants—by increasing their show of affection and support and by helping their partners in various ways. Women tend to respond by improving their physical appearance.

Jealousy is such a powerful tool for reinforcing romantic relationships that some people evoke it on purpose. They will purposely flirt with others, feign lack of interest in their partners and give other signals of being interested in potential rivals. In a study, David Buss found that women reported that the main reason they evoked jealousy in their mates was to increase their partners' commitment. And women who used this strategy were more likely to keep the commitment of their mates. He also found that women who were more involved than their partners in the relationship were more likely to use this strategy than women who were less involved than their partners.[3]

Like all the "negative" emotions, jealousy can be used for good or evil. It can be an early warning signal that some aspects of a love relationship need to be clarified and worked out more thoroughly. It may serve to draw attention to differences in the assumptions and expectations of the partners, to changing assumptions or the need to revise the couple's implicit agreements.

Jealousy can also help us get in touch with the truth of behavior that gets in our way—irrational longings and desires for unconditional love, our desire to have power over other people.

But when it goes awry, jealousy is extremely dangerous. It can corrode marriages, undermine self-esteem, trigger battering and lead to the ultimate crime of murder. One study found that jealousy was the underlying motive in 23 percent of the two hundred murders that were investigated.[4]

Jealousy can be very useful in building a life for yourself. But it needs to be managed carefully. Here is an exercise which I hope will be useful.

Jealousy Exercise

When you feel the pangs of jealousy, find a quiet place to sit or a remote road on which to walk and ask yourself these questions:

- What is it that I want and don't have?
- What can I do to get it?
- Is my love relationship being threatened or somehow in jeopardy? (If you feel that it is, it probably is. You have probably picked up some cues that something is not going right, that your mate is wavering.)
- What do I want to do to protect my love relationship?

Take action in a prudent and balanced way.

Chapter 7

SADNESS

Sadness is beneficial because it tells us what is precious, what is important, what we want to protect and what we value. Sadness is associated with loss and the more valuable the thing that is lost, the sadder we feel. When we know what is precious and what is important, it helps us to set priorities and to distinguish the important from the unimportant. Grief is valuable, not only because it gives us time to heal, but also because it confirms for us what we want to develop, cultivate and protect. This is the value of letting the sadness in and sitting with it.

Perhaps this is why it is helpful to encourage someone who is grieving over the loss of an important person in his or her life to remember that person, recall specific stories and savor the details of the relationship. Such remembering will motivate us to take more care in our relationships with people who are still alive. Any loss brings on sadness; the sadness tells us that what was lost was precious and motivates us to protect and nurture that in the future.

During his freshman year in college, Jeffrey Wilson's older brother died suddenly and his parents divorced. Wilson came home to an empty house. He was grieving. Suffering a lack of energy, deep sadness and the emptiness of loss, he went to a doctor. The doctor prescribed an antidepressant drug. Concerned about the side effects of the drug, Wilson went back to the doctor and the doctor prescribed another drug. Wilson spent the next seventeen years on a cocktail of antidepressants, mood stabilizers and antipsychotic drugs. During that time, he managed to hold down a responsible job, get married and build a family, but he knew that the drugs were keeping him from being who he was and being as healthy as he could be. It took him seven months to wean himself from the drugs. When he did, he realized how much the drugs had cost him in terms of his ability to experience life fully. He wrote a book called *Irrational Medicine* and went on a speaking tour to promote it.

Wilson was the victim of a dangerous trend that I believe is underway in our country. It is the movement to "medicalize" human experience. It used to be that people were shy; now they have social anxiety disorder. We used to say that they were volatile and mercurial; now they have bipolar disorder. It used to be that some children were seen as different, unique, strange in some way; now they are diagnosed with autism spectrum.

When they are diagnosed, it is more than likely that people will be prescribed a psychotropic drug. The majority of the mental health care in the United States is provided by primary care doctors in the form of drugs.[1]

These drugs are not helpful in addressing the cause of the symptoms. They impair the ability of the person to feel and think clearly, increase the risk of dangerous states of being such as akathisia (extreme restlessness and agitation) and mania and increase the risk of suicide, violence, obesity, diabetes and heart disease. If pregnant women take them, the drugs increase the risk of birth defects.

Worst of all, they keep people from getting the messages and learning the lessons from the emotions they are experiencing. Drugs get in the way of this intricate, fine-tuned mechanism that has been evolving for millions of years to help us become aware of concerns that we have and do something about them.

The psychiatrists who are writing the fifth edition of the *Diagnostic and Statistical Manual of Mental Disorders* are discussing the possibility of including grief within two months of a major loss as a mental disorder. If that happens, I believe more and more people will be diagnosed and prescribed drugs that will keep them from experiencing grief and sadness in a way that will be helpful to them.

We are all unique. Each of us experiences grief and sadness in a different way and over a different period of time. There is no formula. The loss of a child or spouse can trigger grief that lasts for one or two years. We want to help people stay alive and gradually be able to resume their roles in life as they go through the grieving process, but there are ways other than drugging them in which we can do that. One thing I suggest is that they read a wonderful book by Melba Colgrove titled *How to Survive the Loss of a Love.* Additionally, in the first days of people's shock, we can bring them food, help them keep house and take over their practical duties so they can go through the most intense part of the process. As time goes on, we can continue to support them and help them remember those who have been lost.

It's important to keep in mind that sadness can be brought on by the loss of something other than a person. What if something has happened to trigger a loss of security, safety or certainty? Perhaps we have lost a job or financial security. We may be concerned about losing some closeness in our love relationship. An injury or sickness can cause a loss of ability to do things which had been enjoyable and profitable in the past. These can all trigger grief and sadness.

The grief and sadness won't be with us forever. Time can heal wounds. If we allow ourselves to experience it, grief and sadness will tell us in a visceral way what is important to us and what we want to nurture, protect and grow as we continue building our lives.

Sadness Exercise

• When you are aware of grief and sadness, let yourself settle into it. Let these feelings wash over you. Get some help from your friends so that you can disconnect for a while. Allow yourself to spend time sitting in quiet reflection, walking by yourself or with a friend. Give yourself permission to cry, take warm baths, spend time in quiet reflection.

- When you're ready, spend some time remembering in depth and detail the person who has been lost, looking at pictures, sharing memories with others or recalling the feeling of security, safety and certainty that has been lost.

- Think about what you want to do to nurture, protect and develop those people, qualities and things that are important to you as you move forward in your life.

Chapter 8

GUILT

G uilt tells us what we don't want to do. It keeps us from hurting other people. It is crucial in enabling us to become better people, more loving, kind, considerate and helpful to others. Guilt is perhaps the emotion which most clearly drives human beings to become better in their treatment of other human beings. It seems to me that our species has become better at that over the past thousand years. There is still a lot of killing going on. But the geographical area in which hurting or killing another person is punishable by law has been steadily expanding. We are much more humane in our treatment of mentally ill people than we were even a hundred years ago. In our country we have made great progress in overcoming unjust discrimination against people of a different color, ethnicity, national origin or sexual orientation. To some extent, we can thank guilt for this progress.

People who don't feel guilt are scary and dangerous. Psychiatrist and author M. Scott Peck has gone so far as to define evil as people who don't own their imperfections. If you don't feel guilty, you can't get better, you can't make amends, you can't atone. My reaction to people who complain about feeling guilty is to say, "If you don't want to feel guilty, don't do things that make you feel guilty." Of course, it's not as easy as that, because the forces that make us do things that produce guilt are powerful drives that are hardwired in us: the drive to mate with whom we want to mate and with more than one member of the opposite sex, to eat what we want to eat, to sleep where we want to sleep, to defend our territory, to protect our loved ones, to do what we want to do when we want to do it, to survive. These are powerful forces and they can lead us to do things that make us feel guilty. The best we can do is manage those drives in ways that enable us to live in civilized society and not let guilt become excessive, unreasonable and hurtful to us. This is not an easy task; for most of us it is a lifelong work in progress.

I think guilt is a very useful emotion. It tells us when we have done wrong and keeps us from continuing to do so. It helps protect our relationships and enhance our social ties. It leads us to be aware of our shortcomings, admit our faults and make amends. Such corrective action repairs the damage to our social ties and our valued relationships. But guilt can be very damaging. It can tie us down to the past, making it difficult for us to live in the authentic present. It can undermine the faith we have in the adequacy of ourselves and lead to loss of self-esteem and self-confidence. It can rob life of its joys and lead to social paralysis. It can damage our relationships and create a breach between ourselves and others. Under the weight of guilt, we feel at a loss to know how to behave in public and to show ourselves as we are.

So what do we do with guilt? How do we manage it so that it helps and doesn't hurt? The first step is to stop denying your guilt. Some people are so hurt by guilt that they become allergic to the feeling. They won't let it in. You may deny guilt by putting it out of your conscious mind, but it will seek partial outlets in various ways. You may try to dispel your guilt by projecting it onto others, such as blaming another employee when you fail at a task at work or blaming your spouse when you do not feel sexually aroused.

Denial of guilt can lead to inauthentic resolution of guilt. You feel guilty, but you try to wriggle out of it instead of coming to terms with it. Or it remains lodged in the unconscious and causes anxiety, depression or distress that seems unexplained. You may minimize the impact of your hurtful behavior, demean the victim, admit guilt but not make amends or deny that you intended to hurt the victim. The problem with inauthentic resolution of guilt is that the damaged relationship is not repaired; rather, it is further undermined.

The first step in authentic resolution of guilt is accepting it, facing it and taking responsibility. But how do we know if our guilt is justified? How do we know if it is reasonable for us to feel guilty? Perhaps we are being too hard on ourselves, falling prey to irrational or excessive guilt, not being compassionate enough with ourselves.

This is what makes guilt so tricky. Much of our guilt may be driven by childhood fantasies—to be loved unconditionally, to be all-powerful and perfect, to get revenge against those who hurt us or get in our way. There is nothing wrong with those fantasies as long as we see them for what they are and admit that some part of them still lurks within us. We would do well to know the difference between fantasies and desires and deeds. There's a part of us that wants to control other people, be sexual giants, do whatever we want to do. But wanting is different from doing; desires are different from deeds.

In our culture, many parents and teachers have instilled beliefs in us that may be causing guilt that is excessive or unreasonable. The advent of safe birth control methods has greatly reduced the danger of premarital sex leading to out-of-wedlock births, thus making such sexual behavior much less irresponsible than it was. We may have been taught that anger is an unacceptable emotion, one that should be extinguished and of which one should be ashamed rather than a useful emotion that can be effectively managed.

One way of knowing whether your guilt is reasonable or not is asking yourself the question: *Am I listening to my own voice or am I listening to the voice of my parents or my culture?* Our parents have tremendous influence over us. We can easily internalize their fears, anger and guilt without being aware of it. I think the fact that I am more vulnerable to guilt is a residue of my father's guilt that is still within me. I once had a therapist who from time to time said to me: "You wouldn't want to be very successful and be disloyal to your father." There are people who feel guilty when they are successful, believing that their parents or siblings will be hurt, will resent them and will, perhaps, attack them.

One way of managing this kind of irrational and excessive guilt is to become good at managing your boundaries. As we will learn in chapter 13, it is dangerous to allow yourself to be too affected by the reactions of other people to your behavior. If you are just living your life the best you can—not trying to hurt anyone else—and other people are having a problem with it, you can let them deal with their reactions. You don't have to take responsibility for their reactions or let them keep you from living your life the way you want to live it.

Once you have done this kind of self-examination, you can trust yourself to know if your guilt is reasonable or not. If it is, you can make amends or take whatever corrective action makes sense.

I think guilt should be mixed with a healthy dose of compassion for yourself. After all, none of us chose our parents. Our parents had control over our early experience in life and that experience determines to a large extent how we behave and how we live our lives. We were dealt a hand of cards. We have some winners and some losers. Whatever we were dealt, we have to play the hand.

Guilt Exercise

When you feel some bodily sensations that you think may be a sign of feeling guilty, ask yourself these questions:

- What might I be feeling guilty about?
- Is this reasonable and justifiable guilt or is it excessive and unreasonable?
- If it is excessive and unreasonable, where is that coming from? Am I listening to my voice or to the voice of my parents or culture?
- If this is reasonable guilt, what am I going to do about it?

Chapter 9

NEGATIVE EMOTIONS
AND GOOD DECISIONS

"Negative" emotions are especially important in helping us to know what we value, what is important to us. It's difficult to know what is valuable through thinking, through using the rational faculty. In order to develop values, we must use our emotions, pay attention to our feelings. It is through this combination of thinking and feeling that we know what is of value to us. There is much focus on teaching character in schools. In order to teach character, people must be taught how to acknowledge, experience and use these "negative" feelings. Schools aren't very good at that and administrators aren't even aware that they're not very good at it.

This ability to combine emotions with reason is crucial to building a good life. In fact, it is very hard to be reasonable if you are not in touch with your feelings, if you don't learn from them. If you can't assign value to different experiences, you will have a hard time making good decisions, decisions that help you live the way you want to live. Antonio Damasio, the medical researcher, studied people who were victims of brain lesions which impeded their abilities to feel. He found that, lacking that ability to feel, people are unable to make good decisions and persist in making destructive investments and bad business and personal decisions, even though in casual conversation they appear to be perfectly normal.[1] Without the use of these "negative" emotions, our rational faculty, the reasoning power that we value so highly, is of little use to us.

Trauma: A barrier to using our feelings

I believe this ability to use all our emotions, especially the "negative" ones, is essential to building a good life. Although we are born with the ability to use these emotions, many of us have not learned how to access them or have forgotten what we once knew. These emotions are fine-tuned mechanisms. The signals from them may be delicate and faint. As in the transmission of radio signals, background noise and static may get in the way of our being able to receive them. Or our receivers may have become so damaged or corroded that we're not able to pick up the signals. What about those of us who live with lots of background noise and static or whose receivers have been so damaged that these signals aren't picked up? What about those of us who have been traumatized?

Trauma creates the kind of noise, static and damaged receivers that get in the way of using our feelings. Trauma victims are unable to use their emotions effectively. They have lost the ability to modulate their emotions. The traumatic experience has taken that ability from them. Trauma victims are afflicted in two ways. On one hand, when visited by an emotion like anger or fear, they may overreact, become excessively activated, spin up to the point of quickly going out of control and lose the ability to control their reactions and behavior. On the other hand, they may react to the first signs of such emotions by shutting down or protecting themselves by retreating into the fuzzy, out-of-touch state that is known clinically as dissociation or depersonalization. They may go out of their bodies and retreat to the extent that they appear to be another person. Reacting in these ways, they not only are unable to use their emotions, but also can't use their rational faculty very well. Trauma is one of the great impediments to living well.

Trauma experts have identified two kinds of trauma: life-threatening trauma and developmental trauma. Life-threatening trauma occurs in rapes, physical assaults and accidents in which the victim faces death. Developmental trauma occurs when a person doesn't receive the kind of nurturance, affirmation, attunement, support and love that human beings need in the first years of their lives. Both kinds of trauma can make it difficult, if not impossible, for the victim to use his or her emotions to live well. It's no accident that trauma victims are significantly more vulnerable to anxiety disorders, mood disorders and psychotic disorders than are other people.

Trauma is devastating. Fortunately, there are numerous therapeutic approaches that have been proven effective in helping trauma victims regain the ability to use their emotions, their bodily sensations and their reasoning abilities: Sensorimotor psychotherapy, eye movement desensitization and reprocessing (EMDR) and other whole-body approaches help victims reprocess the trauma through their bodies, minds and emotions in an integrated way. I encourage anyone who finds him or herself either overreacting or underreacting to powerful emotions to seek and receive treatment from a psychotherapist who has proven experience in treating trauma victims. Such therapy can help trauma victims dislodge the energy that has become frozen in their bodies—all mammals freeze when they are unable to flee or fight against overwhelming force—and slowly learn how to use their bodies, emotions and minds to deal effectively with threat and demand. For a good book on this subject see *Traumatic Stress* by Bessel van der Kolk, Alexander McFarlane and Lars Weisaeth.

Psychotropic drugs: The great disablers

I don't think it is a good idea for most people to use psychotropic drugs of any kind—antidepressants, antianxieties, antipsychotics, mood stabilizers or stimulants. These medications mess around with an incredibly wonderful, fine-tuned, intricate mechanism that has been evolving over eons and which is designed to help human beings respond to threats, solve problems, protect themselves and their loved ones, survive and prosper.

There is a place for psychotropic drugs. If people are in danger of hurting themselves or others and psychotropic drugs will keep them from doing that, it makes sense to use them. But those instances are relatively rare. What is more common is for people to use the drugs because they feel on edge, are feeling down, are anxious, can't function or are experiencing panic attacks. When people use drugs to counteract these kinds of feelings and reactions, they are messing around with their emotional mechanisms and hurting themselves, because they are keeping themselves from using these feelings and reactions to become aware of what is going on in their lives, what is threatening them, what they are afraid of, what they need to deal with and what they need to do to live more the way they want to live. They are cutting themselves off from a wonderful mechanism, the function of which is to help them survive and live well.

If you feel like hiding in your house, not going to work, not talking to anyone and retreating from the world, I believe it could be a signal that you need to take stock of your life, spend some time reflecting about where you are in your life, where you want to go, what it's going to take to get there and what obstacles need to be dealt with. Perhaps this is a wake-up call telling you that life isn't all fun and games, that there is a serious side to it, that this isn't a dress rehearsal, it's the main event, these are the "good old days" and you'd better get on with the task of making the most of it. Why would you want to ignore a wake-up call like that?

There are two kinds of psychotropic medicines: uppers and downers. They either bring your mood up or take you down, artificially energize and activate you or put a damper on you. The people who make and sell psychotropic medication want you to believe that they know more about this than they really do. For example, we hear a lot about chemical imbalances. But nobody has determined what a "chemically balanced" brain consists of. Nobody is able to describe the chemically balanced brain. If you don't know what a balanced brain consists of, you can't detect a chemically imbalanced one.

In fact, drug trials that were used to prove the effectiveness of many antidepressants demonstrated that they were only very slightly more effective than placebos.

But, even if psychotropic medications are proven to be effective in altering mood, I believe that it's not a good idea to use them unless a person is at serious risk of hurting him or herself or others, for three reasons: First, when you use psychotropic drugs you are depriving yourself of the opportunity to learn how to manage yourself and use your emotions, your mind and your bodily sensations to adjust to situations, events, problems, dilemmas, quandaries, opportunities and crises. In terms of the parable about the hungry man, you are being given fish rather than being taught how to fish. This is what good psychotherapy does: it teaches you how to use your resources well and how to manage yourself in the process of living more the way you want to live. It teaches you how to become aware of your wants and your needs and how to find effective ways of satisfying them.

Second, psychotropic drugs impair your ability to use your conscience, your caring to keep from hurting other people. This was a concern of Peter Kramer, the first psychiatrist to write extensively about antidepressants. He found that his clients who were taking antidepressant medicines had lost their abilities to care about their behaviors, had lost that valuable ability that keeps us from doing things we will feel guilty about.[2] Barb, a client of mine, told me that she wouldn't have been able to leave her husband had it not been for her antidepressant medicine. I can see how she appreciated the medicine, but she would have been a lot better off if, with the help of a therapist, she had been able to leave her husband with a clear mind and with the ability to feel the feelings associated with leaving. She would have learned that sometimes, in order to save yourself, you have to hurt other people, not because you want to, but because you have to in order to survive. That is a lesson that she could have used for the rest of her life.

One of the dangerous "side effects" of antidepressants is an increased risk of suicide. From my experience as a psychologist, I learned why this might be true. As I described earlier, psychiatrist Peter Kramer found that clients on antidepressants lost their consciences. They lost their abilities to care about how their behavior affected other people. Whenever clients of mine tell me they are thinking about killing themselves, I ask them what the advantage of that would be. Practically everyone says, "I wouldn't have to feel this pain any more. It would be all over." Then I ask them what the disadvantage of killing themselves would be. Virtually everyone replies, "It would be very hurtful to my family. It would be devastating to them." I think it is this awareness that keeps many people from committing suicide. If the antidepressants take away that concern, it is easier for people to kill themselves. Perhaps that is the source of the increased risk of suicide for people on antidepressants.

Third, psychotropic drugs impair your ability to experience and use certain emotions and states of being. All emotions and states of being are potentially useful. If they weren't, they would have been wiped out by natural selection long ago. What is the usefulness of depression? Depression is useful in numerous important ways. It is a protective reaction of the body/mind to prolonged periods of intense stress. Long periods of stress can cause heart attack, stroke and, by impairing the immune system, cancer. Depression is a way of shutting down and protecting and is a message that something isn't going right. Maybe it's time to stop focusing on success, work and other people and to take stock of what is going on in your life, what isn't right and needs to be addressed. Depression introduces a necessary seriousness and weightiness to life and tells us to become more reflective and mindful. Psychotropic drugs deprive you of the ability to use depression to live more the way you want to live.

Psychotropic medicines can increase the risk of suicide and violence. Both of the boys who killed twelve people at Columbine High School and then committed suicide were taking mind-altering substances. Many people who have opened fire on schools and workplaces have been on psychotropic medicines. There is enough evidence of this to have convinced authorities in the United Kingdom to prohibit the prescription of almost all antidepressants to children and youths and for the United States Food and Drug Administration to require pharmaceutical companies to put a warning on the labels of antidepressant drugs. This is not to mention the serious side effects such as tremors and sexual dysfunction that accompany the use of these medications and the fact that some people experience great difficulty in withdrawing from them.

The final irony here is that the psychotropic drugs that are prescribed by psychiatrists work in the same way that illegal drugs—heroin, cocaine, methamphetamines—work. All mind-altering drugs work by either enhancing or depressing the function of the receptors of neurotransmitters in the brain. They either inhibit or facilitate the reuptake of neurotransmitters. The only difference between a prescribed antidepressant and cocaine is that the antidepressant inhibits the reuptake of serotonin while cocaine inhibits the reuptake of a whole host of neurotransmitters including norepinephrine, noradrenalin, dopamine, gabamentin, etc.

Here are some exercises to help you become more aware of your feelings, more friendly toward them and more able to use them for your benefit.

Becoming Friendly With Your Feelings

As you go through the rest of today, pay attention to your feelings. When you are aware that you are experiencing a feeling, let yourself know it. Instead of fighting it off, let the feeling in, even if for only several moments. Give it a name and make a preliminary guess as to what it is about, where it is coming from. Then, when you have the time and space to do it, find a quiet place where you can be alone and ask yourself these questions:

- Where is this feeling coming from?
- What is this feeling telling me about myself, my situation, what I like, what I don't like, what is important to me?
- What can I learn from this feeling?
- How can I use the energy from this feeling to do something that will help me live more the way I want to live?

Write an account of this experience. It can be a few sentences or a few paragraphs.

Controlled Catharsis: Getting in Touch and Letting It Out

The next time you find yourself unable to sleep, waking up at one or two in the morning and not being able to go back to sleep, suffering from panic attacks during the day or being plagued by obvious signs of stress, find a place where you can be alone, alone enough so that people won't hear or see what you're doing. Get a pillow or a cushion and start beating it, hitting it. Begin at your own pace. If you find that you want to say something or make a sound as you hit the pillow, do it. Let yourself get into whatever rhythm, level of effort, vigorousness, loudness or verbosity that comes to you. Close your eyes and see if you can bring up an image of what or whom you are angry with. Continue for as long as you want. When you are ready to stop, stop. Gradually wind down, sit in a quiet place and focus on the feelings that were elicited by the exercise.

Continue to sit quietly and relaxed and begin saying, "Right now I am aware of..." and finish the sentence with your own words. Continue doing this until you no longer want to do it.

Alternatives include finding a place in nature in which you are alone, picking up a stick and hitting a rock or the ground;

finding a quiet, country road, walking down it and talking to yourself as you walk; using a punching bag to work out on.

Write a brief account of your experience in doing this exercise.

Connecting Your Feelings and Your Thoughts

This is an exercise that will help you use your feelings to inform and guide your thinking.

1. **Relaxing and Quieting Down**

   Take a moment to relax. One simple and effective way of relaxing is to find a comfortable chair and sit in it. As you sit, allow the tension to drip slowly out of your body. As you begin to quiet down, focus your attention on your breathing. Just notice your breathing, the steady in and out of your stomach, the feeling of breath passing through your nose or mouth. As you sit focusing your attention on your breathing, you will notice thoughts coming into your head. That is fine. There is no way to keep your mind from working. But what you can do is not hold onto the thoughts. Just notice them and then let them go. Like clouds moving through the sky, let your thoughts come into your head, notice them, let them go and bring your focus back to your breathing. Now pay attention inwardly, inside your body, perhaps in your stomach or chest. See what comes there when you ask, *How is my life going? What is the main thing for me right now?* Sense within your body. Let the answers come slowly from this sensing. When some concern comes, *do not dwell on it.* Stand back, say to yourself, *Yes, that's there. I can feel that.* Put it to the side. Then ask what else you feel. Wait again and sense. Usually there are several things.

2. **Feeling the Problem**

   From among what came up, select one personal problem to focus on. Stand back from it. There are many parts to that one thing you are thinking about—too many to think of each one alone. But you can feel all of these things together. Pay attention in your body where you usually feel things and you can get a sense of what all of the problems feel like. Let yourself feel the sense of all of that. It may not be clear, but let yourself feel whatever it is.

3. **Giving the Feeling a Name**

   What is the quality of this unclear feeling? Let a word, a phrase or an image come up from the feeling itself. It might be a quality word, like tight, sticky, scary, stuck, heavy, jumpy or a phrase or an image. Stay with the quality of the feeling until something fits it just right.

4. **Relating the Feeling and the Word or Phrase**

   Go back and forth between the feeling and the word, phrase or image. Check how they relate to each other. See if there is a bodily signal that lets you know there is a fit. To do it, you have to have the feeling there again as well as the word. Let the feeling change, if it does, and also the word or picture until they feel just right in capturing the quality of the feeling.

5. **Asking**

   Now ask yourself: *What is it about this whole problem that makes this so…?* Insert the word, phrase or image that has come to you. Make sure you sense the quality freshly, vividly (not just remembered from before). When it is there again, tap it, touch it, be with it, asking, *What is it that brings this feeling? What would it take for it to feel better?* When you get an answer to these questions you may feel a shift, a slight "give" or release. Now ask yourself: *What are some next steps I can take to deal with this problem or to move in the direction I want to move?*

6. **Receiving**

   Receive whatever thoughts or ideas come up in a friendly way. Stay with them for a while. Pay attention to them, even if they don't make a lot of sense. Whatever comes, this is just a start; there will be other thoughts, ideas and steps to take.

If at some point during this exercise you have spent a little while sensing and touching an unclear, holistic bodily sense of this problem, then you have connected the feelings and the thoughts. It doesn't matter whether the body shift came or not. It comes on its own. We can't control that.

Chapter 10

STRESS:
THE GREAT ENABLER

"Stress" has become the verbal currency of popular psychology. It has been featured on countless magazine covers, on TV shows and in pop psychology books. Like most things which become wildly popular, it has been misunderstood and misused. The term *stress* was coined in the 1950s by Hans Selye, a medical researcher in Montreal. Selye defined stress as "the nonspecific response of the organism to any demand placed upon it."[1]

Selye came to see stress as a marvelous physiological reaction of the human organism to threat and demand, a reaction that had evolved over the eons and enabled humans to survive as a species. Far from being a hostile force, Selye saw it as a key to human adaptation. The only way to avoid stress is to be dead, he said. But, like many things, it was very helpful at the right times and in the right amounts and very dangerous if it persisted over long stretches of time or was too intense. Selye made a distinction between what he called *eustress*—the stress reaction that is helpful and functional—and *distress*—the stress reaction that is harmful and dysfunctional.[2] Thus, the stress response is a complicated process: when it is used appropriately, it enables us to address the challenges that we must address in order to live as we want to live; when used inappropriately or not at all, it causes disease and death.

In a fascinating study of baboons, scientist Robert Sapolsky discovered that the same is true of our primate cousins. He found that some baboons had better biochemistry than others. The ones with the good biochemistry experienced stress reactions appropriately and used them to address challenges. The ones with bad biochemistry were under more constant, unmodulated and unused stress and were not as effective at addressing challenges. In fact, the baboons with good biochemistry who had appropriate stress reactions were different from those with bad biochemistry in certain ways:

1. They were very good at detecting the difference between real and unreal threats.

2. When faced with a real threat they took control, either by confronting the challenge or by getting away from it.

3. When they lost confrontations, you could tell by their behavior that they had lost. In other words, they behaved appropriately based on the outcomes of the confrontations.

4. When they lost, they displaced aggression onto third parties, i.e., weaker and lower status baboons.[3]

If we modify the last point slightly to advise the redirection of aggression into sports, building things and other creative activities rather than hurting other people, these would be good rules for humans to follow in managing stress. They focus on the threat or demand that is causing the stress, they make a distinction between real and perceived threats, they emphasize the importance of being realistic about the threat and one's response to it and they acknowledge that something has to be done with the energy associated with the stress response or it will cause harm to oneself or others.

Learning to use the stress response

How do you know you're experiencing a stress response? Immediately, you'll feel like you're getting armed for battle. You'll feel one or a combination of these reactions:

- The rush of your heart pumping faster and harder
- Queasiness and tension in the pit of your stomach
- Tightness in your head or around your head
- A feeling of energy in your muscles
- Lightheadedness

But if you don't notice these symptoms or don't do anything with the energy in them, after a while you'll begin to experience other symptoms:

- Fatigue, irritability and nervousness
- Trouble concentrating
- Sleeplessness or a desire to sleep all the time
- Lack of appetite or a desire to eat all the time
- Anger without knowing why, a desire to lash out at people for no apparent reason
- Pain throughout your body
- Arms and legs going to sleep
- Headaches
- Upset stomach
- Shortness of breath
- Dizziness

Dr. Selye's prescription for dealing with stress is to identify the threat or demand that is causing it, turn the threat or demand into a problem that can be solved and work at solving it. This, I think, is the basis for good stress management. The necessary first step is to figure out what is causing the stress. What is the threat or demand that you are responding to, think you may have to respond to or think you should be responding to? What is it that you need to do that is going to be hard? Sometimes it is easy to figure that out; sometimes it is very difficult. It can be difficult, because once you know what is causing the threat, you are going to be compelled to either do something about it or decide that you are going to try to live with it. That is a tough decision. If you decide to do something about it, you are probably in for a battle, because if it were going to be easy to deal with, you probably would have already dealt with it.

Are you loving and working in the ways you want to? If your answer to that crucial question is *No*, then ask yourself: *What is getting in the way of my loving and working in the way I want to?* or *What do I need to do in order to love and work the way I want to?* (When I use the word *work* in the context of stress management, I am talking about how we express ourselves, how we use our minds, bodies, hearts, voices, creativity and problem-solving abilities. Some people are able to do this at their jobs. Those who aren't have to find ways of expressing themselves outside of their jobs—in the evenings, on weekends, on vacation.)

These are key questions, because human beings have an innate drive to love and work as they want to. Anything that gets in the way of that drive will be perceived as a threat and will cause a stress response. Since the drive to love and work is innate, you don't have much choice over whether you express it or not. It's not as if you can easily say, *Oh well, I'll just have to learn to live without loving and working the way I want to.* You may override those drives and learn to live without expressing them, but you run a great risk of paying a price in terms of your health and well-being.

Your honest answers to the questions will help you identify the threat or demand which is causing the stress in your life. Identifying the threat is a crucial first step in managing stress. Now comes the hard part, because what is getting in the way and causing the threat is probably another person, a moral principle or rule that you have decided to live by or some fear, inability, deficit or block inside yourself. It takes courage to be willing to know what is causing the threat or demand and what has to be dealt with. Dealing with it is going to be difficult, uncomfortable and *stressful*. In order to deal with the threat that is causing the harmful distress in your life, you are going to have to use the energy from the stress response. That is why the First Principle of Stress Management is: Never seek comfort or avoid discomfort.

If you seek comfort, you won't deal with the threat or demand that is causing the harmful and uncomfortable stress in your life. You will get comfort in the short run but a lot of discomfort in the long run.

It is very important that you honor the First Principle of Stress Management. Some people may have been exposed to stress management techniques that focus on reframing the threat, thinking yourself out of it. This is the "Don't sweat the small stuff—and it's all small stuff" approach to stress management. For the small number of people who tend to exaggerate threats or see a threat where none is there, this may be a good approach. But for most of us it is very dangerous, because *some stuff is not small stuff*. Loving and working the way you want to love and work is not small stuff. If you don't deal with the small stuff, it will become big stuff and then you have more stress and difficulty with which to deal. Not dealing with the small stuff can lead to a world of hurt. It also won't work to avoid stress. If you try to avoid it, you won't be addressing the threat or taking the action that is being demanded of you and you'll be under even worse stress.

Recent research demonstrates the danger of avoiding stress. Studies on the impact of different coping methods on physical and mental health have found that people who use denial ("I've been saying to myself, 'This isn't real.'"), self-distraction ("I've been turning to work or other activities to take my mind off things."), self-blame ("I've been criticizing myself.") or alcohol and drugs have poorer mental and physical health than people who use active coping ("I've been taking action to try and make the situation better.").[4]

Respected psychotherapist Friedrich "Fritz" Perls had an insight that fits well here. He found that people often have a fairly good idea of what they want or need, but they then interrupt or stop themselves. By continually stopping themselves they fail to achieve closure on getting what they want or need and become burdened by a lot of unfinished business. The accumulation of unfinished business eventually drags them down and results in disease.[5]

Perls believed that healthy living results from effectively managing a constant cycle in which you become aware of a need or want, act effectively to meet it and then lapse back into rest until becoming aware of another want or need. He called it the Cycle of Experience.[6]

The cycle starts with the person at rest. At some point he or she notices a bodily sensation arising and becomes aware of a need or want which is associated with the sensation. Energy begins to build up in him or her. He or she uses the energy to take action. If he or she acts effectively, he or she gets into contact with the need or want and satisfies it. He or she achieves closure and returns to rest until becoming aware of another sensation.

Any break in the cycle or difficulty in addressing one of the steps will be experienced as painful or problematic and will create a stress response. Continual inability to meet needs or wants (a buildup of unfinished business) will eventually result in stress that is unmanaged and becomes locked up in the body, where it results in disease and illness.

There are many ways in which people stop themselves. One way is by "adding to" or "subtracting from" reality. Adding to reality includes irrational fears or beliefs that keep a person from using his or her energy to take effective action to meet the need or want. Subtracting from reality includes the kind of denial or repression which keeps a person from noticing the sensations that trigger awareness of need or want. These blocks are very amenable to therapeutic approaches which help people become aware of the ways in which they stop themselves and teach people how to overcome them.

What can you do to use this therapeutic approach?

Becoming Aware of How You Stop Yourself

- If you find yourself becoming frustrated, angry or stressed, ask yourself if there is a lot of unfinished business piling up.

- If there is, work at becoming aware of how you are stopping yourself from addressing wants and needs and finishing business. Be especially careful about thoughts that you use to stop yourself which are not objective or realistic (see chapter 4 for a better understanding of such distorted thinking and how to counter it).

- If you become aware that you are misusing thoughts in ways that are stopping you from meeting important needs and wants, use the Fear Exercise in chapter 4 to check your thinking and find ways of overcoming irrational and unrealistic thoughts.

- Since we are often stopped by a fear of hurting other people or incurring their wrath, refer to the techniques in chapter 13 for relating effectively with others without giving up too much of yourself.

Once you have identified the threat to your ability to love and work as you want to, you will decide whether or not to address it. In either case, you will be under considerable stress. You may decide for various reasons that you don't want to address it at this time—not because you are seeking comfort and avoiding discomfort but for strategic or practical reasons. For example, you may find that your job is keeping you from working in the way that you want to and that there is nothing you can do about changing it in the short run. You need the income and you don't want to change jobs, because it will be damaging to your children and/or spouse. Or you may be having trouble in your marriage. You know you're going to have to do something about it at some point, but now is not the time. So you are stuck for the time being. But at least you know what is causing the stress in your life. You have made some progress, but you're still going to be living with lots of stress.

On the other hand, you may decide to address the threat. This means that you are going to have to do some things which are uncomfortable, scary and likely to be very stressful. This is a dilemma. If you decide not to address the threat, you are going to be living with it and, therefore, experiencing high levels of stress. And, if you decide to address it, you're going to be facing the stress associated with taking uncomfortable and scary action and running into the inevitable roadblocks, hiatuses and disappointments along the way. It's time to use the Second Principle of Stress Management: Use the energy in the stress response. Here is a list of some ways to do that:

Use the Energy in the Stress Response

1. Find a creative activity in which to engage. This might be some artistic work, building something, creating an organization or contributing to an already existing one or engaging in competitive sports.
2. Get some vigorous exercise every day. Spend at least thirty minutes *every day* running, aerobic walking, swimming, bicycle riding, rowing or doing some other activity that gets your heart rate up to 80 percent of maximum. If you feel too tired to do it, do it anyway. You'll feel a lot more energetic after you do. If you haven't been exercising at all, start slowly—do it for five minutes and then increase it the next day.
3. Engage in some kind of relaxation practice. This can include meditation, yoga or simple relaxation exercises.
4. Talk with a friend, confidant, counselor, therapist, clergyman or spouse about the threat with which you are dealing. Find someone who is willing to listen and encourage you to talk without trying to solve your problem for you.
5. Find a place where you can scream and/or pound on something. The car is good for this. You can find a secluded spot to park the car or walk deep into the woods or desert beyond the reach of civilization. When you're doing this,

know that it is totally normal, natural and healthy to have that kind of rage in you and to express it in that way.

6. Do some kind of volunteering that involves helping people directly: working at a soup kitchen or homeless shelter, coaching children, candy-striping at a hospital.

7. Spend some time writing about traumatic experiences you have suffered and/or things that are upsetting you, threatening you or embarrassing you. Explore your deepest thoughts and feelings and why you feel the way you do. Write about your "negative" feelings such as sadness, hurt, anger, hate, fear and guilt. Write about the most emotionally painful experiences of your life. Don't edit or worry about how it sounds or that it might be petty, selfish or stupid.

Know what you want

It's impossible to do a good job of managing stress if you don't know what you want. If you don't know what you want, you won't know what is threatening you or the action that is being demanded of you. Knowing what you want does not come easily in our society. We are taught that it is not really okay to want. It's okay to need but not to want. Wanting is selfish. But I know that if you get what you want, other people are going to get what they want, because one of the things you want is to love the way you want to love. If you start loving the way you want to love and expressing yourself the way you want to express yourself, other people are going to benefit.

I believe the biggest failure of our schools is that they do not teach children how to know what they want and desire and how to manage themselves so they can get what they want and desire without hurting or being insensitive to other people. This is a key part of emotional intelligence and I feel that it is utterly ignored in our schools.

You can't know what you want by using only your mind. You can only know by using both your mind and your body. If you try to figure it out in your head, it won't work. Knowing what you want is a visceral process; you feel it in your body. If you're in touch with your body, you can become aware of it and then it appears as a thought in your mind.

Here is an exercise designed to help you take that crucial first step in managing your stress:

Stress Management Action Plan

These questions are designed to help you develop a Stress Management Action Plan.

1. What is threatening my ability to love and work (express myself) the way I want to? What is being demanded of me that is going to be hard to do?
2. What, if anything, do I want to do about it? If I decide not to do anything about it, how will I use the energy in the stress in healthy ways?
3. What is going to be hard about doing something about it? What concerns do I have?
4. What can I do to address these concerns?
5. What is my plan of action?
6. Since implementing the plan is going to take time and is going to be stressful, how will I use the energy in the stress in healthy ways?

In the process of managing your stress, you will be helping your spouses, parents, children, friends, colleagues, bosses, customers, etc., because the key to managing your stress is finding ways of loving and working as you want. As you build your capacity to love and work as you want to, your fellow humans will benefit; as you become healthier, you serve others.

Chapter 11

USE "NEGATIVE" THINKING

Here's the good news: You have a wonderful brain that you can use to make sense out of things, plan your future, analyze complicated situations, make decisions, create, imagine and build.

Here's the bad news: You have a wonderful brain that you can use to create thoughts that make you feel bad, keep you from doing what you want to do and aid you in doing what you shouldn't do.

By now most of you know how this amazingly flexible and adaptable organ can make you feel miserable and get you into trouble. You've probably had thoughts like these:

- I'll never learn to do this.
- I'm just no good.
- I'll never be as good as _____.
- I'd better not bring that up, because if I do, things will just get worse.
- Let's face it: I'm a nobody/loser/jerk.
- I've taken enough of this. S/he's going to have to make the first move.
- People are just mean, selfish, competitive, prejudiced, insensitive, dense, stupid, etc. It's no use. I'm just going to lie low for a while or I'll find a way to get back at him or her.
- I wonder why s/he's angry with me (when I am actually angry with him or her).

- It's my own fault. If I were smarter, braver, stronger, more loving, less impulsive, etc., that wouldn't have happened.
- Things are out of my control. There's nothing I can do about them.
- What do they expect from me? I never had a chance. I was handicapped from the start.
- Things never work out the way I want them to. It's really no use trying.
- I should do/be better.
- I shouldn't have done that/been like that.
- I'm too afraid to do that.

The incredible distortion machine

What is the function of this kind of thinking? Remember, one of the basic messages of this book is that all of our experiences are there for a reason and are potentially useful.

One possibility is that these thoughts are accurate. Perhaps we really aren't very good, are at fault, are angry with someone, are seeing the ugliness of the world as it really is. If so, it's helpful to know the truth and not be in denial. As the saying goes, "Just because you're paranoid doesn't mean somebody isn't really after you."

More often than not, these kinds of thoughts are distortions, exaggerations, misinterpretations. What is their function? How do we use them?

Perhaps these painful, uncomfortable thoughts are designed to make us right. If we've been told that we're no good, undeserving, essentially bad and that we shouldn't be wrong, these negative thoughts can make us right, which is what we want to be, even if it makes us feel bad.

These thoughts can keep us from being winners and having to suffer the attacks of people who don't like winners. One of my therapists used to remind me regularly that people like losers. They like people who aren't threatening and who aren't better than they are. As soon as you start to be a winner and to be very successful, many people are going to start taking shots at you to bring you down. These kinds of thoughts can keep you from being a winner and make you subject to such attacks.

You can use these kinds of thoughts as an excuse for not trying hard and running the risk that, even if you put tremendous effort into something, you may not succeed. Thus, they can protect you from disappointment. One of the most successful men I know told me: "Al, I didn't succeed until I was willing to fail." What he meant is that he took away all the excuses. He put in so much effort and took so much risk that, if he failed, his only explanation was that he wasn't good enough. That takes courage.

Thoughts such as, *It's no use. It will never work. If I confront him or her, it will make things worse* can be used to avoid risk, to avoid taking the chance that somebody won't like you or will be mad at you. Some people would rather be miserable than be disliked or considered selfish and difficult. Thoughts like, *He or she is useless or not worth it* can make one feel superior, even at the expense of being lonely and separated. Maybe we use these thoughts to keep from trying and failing once again. That would certainly be understandable.

Sometimes we use distorted thinking to avoid feeling guilty or bad. Here are two examples:

A man decided that he wanted a divorce from his wife. It wasn't really because of anything she had done or not done. He was just tired of being married and wanted the excitement and adventure of a single life. But he wouldn't hurt his wife unless she deserved it. So he made up reasons for her to deserve it: She didn't wear sexy enough clothes. She didn't keep the house clean enough. He didn't like her friends. She didn't understand him. Instead of being honest with her, he created reasons why she deserved to be hurt.

The second example is one that occurs often in organizations:

John and Ted had been working together in the nuclear power plant for many years. They had worked their way up through the ranks. John was the plant manager and Ted was in charge of the control room operators, the director of operations. Rich was the "golden boy" in the organization, the one who had been picked by the vice president for nuclear operations to be his successor. Rich had been off on a sabbatical, visiting and working in other nuclear plants and at the Nuclear Regulatory Commission in Washington. He was now ready to return to work in the plant. The logical place to put him was director of operations, the job that Ted was filling. Had John been honest and up front, he would have gone to Ted and said something like: "Ted, we're going to do a horrible thing to you. We're going to do something to you that you don't deserve. We're going to move you to training and give operations to Rich. It's not right, but it's what the vice president wants to do. He's grooming Rich for the vice presidency and this is the next step up for Rich." Instead, John made up a bunch of reasons why Ted was being removed: Ted didn't have the respect of the operators. He had made some management mistakes. He wasn't decisive enough. They were bogus explanations, but they enabled John and the vice president to fool themselves into thinking that Ted deserved to be replaced. This inability or unwillingness to be honest with Ted ruined a friendship that had been forged over a decade of working together and, paradoxically, was more hurtful to Ted than if he had been told the truth.

Sometimes, painful and so-called "negative" thinking is absolutely essential. As I mentioned previously, M. Scott Peck, the psychiatrist author of *The Road Less Traveled*, defines evil as people who don't own their imperfections, who won't or can't accept and acknowledge their faults. That is a painful thing to do. But if people don't own their imperfections, they can't get better. They continue to hurt other people and, ultimately, themselves.

"Negative thinking" is not always dysfunctional. Sometimes it is a crucial part of knowing the truth about yourself, a key to living well. And sometimes it is a key to knowing the situation you are in and especially to knowing what is threatening you and what action is being demanded of you. In the chapter on stress management, I warned you of the danger of thinking yourself out of dealing with the threats you need to deal with or avoiding the action that you need to take. Remember the First Principle of Stress Management: Never seek comfort or avoid discomfort. If you use your thoughts to be comfortable, you may think yourself out of confronting the obstacles that are in your way and resign yourself to living with them. Or you may try to think yourself out of the uncomfortable feelings which are the beacons that you need to acknowledge and follow. Most stress management seminars and articles emphasize this idea of changing your thinking about the stress. But one harmful consequence of that approach is that it may lead you to ignore the fact that there is some real threat to your ability to love and work which you need to address or, at least, acknowledge and find a way to live with.

There is another kind of "negative thinking" that, if explored, can be very useful. It is the thinking that makes one depressed: *My life is a mess. Nothing is going right. I'm in big trouble.* Sometimes this thinking is very useful, because it tells you that your life is not going well. Something is wrong with it. You are headed in the wrong direction. You don't like the way it is going and you don't see any way out. This is a wake-up call that needs to be heeded. And some of the symptoms of depression—wanting to avoid the world, to go inside oneself, to retreat—may be helpful in heeding that wake-up call.

If you use the approach outlined in this book, the quietness, emptiness, inwardness and sadness of depression can help you get in touch with the seriousness and weightiness of life and become more aware of impending death. Being more aware of the reality of death can introduce a certain urgency into life, a realization that you won't be here forever and that there are things you want to do before you leave. The focusing inside of depression can help you learn from your memories, take stock of your life and, perhaps, make a mid-course correction. It can help you learn more about yourself and become familiar with the weighty, dark, serious, reflective side of yourself that you have been avoiding.

Depression can help you get in touch with the necessary regrets of life. How could we not have regrets? Every time we decide to do one thing, we also decide *not* to do a hundred things that we would like to do and which might be quite profitable and enjoyable. One of the hardest things about life is that we can't do all the things we want to do or could imagine doing. Better to acknowledge and experience that regret than to imagine it isn't there or shouldn't be there.

Evolutionary psychologists are beginning to ask themselves what might be the value of depression. They reason that anything we can experience must have some survival value. If not, it would have been wiped out by natural selection long ago. Behavioral ecologist Paul Watson thinks that depression is valuable in that it forces people to renegotiate their relationships with people who have power over them. Evolutionary psychologist Edward Hagen surmises that it was useful in hunter-gatherer societies, because it forced members of the tribe to help the one who was depressed.[1] Modern psychologists are beginning to theorize that the rumination that depressed people engage in may be useful in helping them to get in touch with what is wrong and what they want to do about it.

Automatic negative thoughts: A key to knowing yourself

Negative thoughts can also bring us down and make us miserable. They can be irrational and exaggerated. Psychologist Albert Ellis coined the terms *awfulizing*—exaggerating negative events into catastrophes—and *musterbating*—believing that things must be a certain way or that one must behave a certain way to the point of making oneself miserable.[2]

Ellis was interested in how people make a sane statement: "I'm very upset that my girlfriend has broken up with me. I wish that wouldn't have happened. It's going to take me a while to get over it" and then follow it with an insane statement: "I'll never meet anyone like her again. I'll never be in love again. Life isn't worth living without her. I'm going to kill myself."

Ellis came up with a list of common irrational beliefs that create problems for people:[3]

1. It is a dire necessity for an adult human being to be loved or approved of by virtually every significant other person in his community.
2. One should be thoroughly competent, adequate and achieving in all possible respects if one is to consider oneself worthwhile.
3. Certain people are bad, wicked or villainous and they should be severely blamed and punished for their villainy.
4. It is awful and catastrophic when things are not the way one would very much like them to be.
5. Human happiness is externally caused and people have little or no ability to control their sorrows and disturbances.
6. If something is or may be dangerous or fearsome, one should be terribly concerned about it and should keep dwelling on the possibility of its occurring.
7. It is easier to avoid than to face certain life difficulties and self-responsibilities.
8. One should be dependent on others and need someone stronger than oneself on whom to rely.
9. One's past history is an all-important determiner of one's present behavior and, because something once strongly affected one's life, it should indefinitely have a similar effect.
10. One should become quite upset over other people's problems and disturbances.

Psychiatrist Aaron Beck was especially struck by how automatic these thoughts are, how people get in the habit of thinking them and lose track of the idea that they have some choice about what they are thinking. In his work with clients, Dr. Beck helps them become aware of the thoughts, think about where they come from, realize they have some choice about them and find alternative thoughts that are more objective, realistic and helpful.[4]

Over the years, these kinds of thoughts which create problems for people and make them feel bad have been catalogued. Here are some of them:

- **All or Nothing Thinking:** Sometimes called "black and white" thinking. It is the habit of thinking in extremes and refusing to see the complexity of things and is associated with perfectionism. Things are either great or horrible with no in-between.

- **Overgeneralization:** Taking a single negative event and arbitrarily extending it to forever and always. A man asks a woman out, is rebuffed and thinks, *I'll* never *get a date. Women are* always *turning me down.*

- **Selective Negative Focus:** You pick out the negative details in any situation and dwell on them exclusively. A student receives a C on an exam and decides to drop out of school and give up her dream of becoming a writer only to find, upon checking with her professor, that C was an above average grade and that her professor thinks she has great potential.

- **Contaminating the Present:** Bringing things from the past into the present in a harmful way. A woman who continually sabotages herself learns that she is afraid of winning, because as a child, whenever she won her father's love she lost her mother's and vice versa.

- **Discounting the Positive:** A woman is hospitalized with severe depression and believes nobody cares about her. She receives a warm tribute from the staff upon leaving and says, "The only reason they did that was because they're staff in a hospital. No real person outside of the hospital could care about me."

- **Arbitrary Inference:** You jump to a negative conclusion that is not justified by the facts or situation. You assume that other people are looking down on you. You respond by withdrawing or counterattacking, which brings on the very result you imagined.

- **"Should" Statements:** You try to motivate yourself by saying "I *should* do this" or "I *must* do that" and end up feeling pressured, guilty and resentful. Note that these "shoulds" are seldom examined to see if they make sense or are realistic.
- **Labeling:** An extreme form of overgeneralizing in which you create a negative identity for yourself by focusing on errors and imperfections. There is a good chance you are doing this when you describe yourself with sentences like "I am a _____ kind of person."
- **Personalization:** You relate a negative event to yourself when there is no basis for doing so. Your child does poorly in school and you blame it on your failure as a parent without examining all of the other possible explanations.

This is very confusing and difficult. Sometimes you need to pay attention to these negative and painful thoughts and use them for your benefit. Sometimes you need to realize that they are keeping you from doing what you should do, just another way of punishing yourself or making you do things that you shouldn't do. How do you know the difference?

One way of doing that is to check your thoughts with someone whom you consider to have a fairly good grasp on reality. Another is to check for evidence. See yourself as a scientist who is going to base conclusions, attributions, assertions and beliefs on an objective appraisal of facts, data and information. Try out some alternative hypotheses that might be just as good explanations as the one you have fixed on.

We need to be careful about what we are thinking. We need to realize that we have a choice about what we think. We think what we think for all kinds of reasons, many of which don't have anything to do with what is rational, objective or realistic.

There's no easy answer to this need to distinguish between the negative thoughts you need to pay attention to and the ones you need to notice but not follow. Here is an exercise designed to help you deal with this difficulty:

Monitoring and Managing Your Thoughts

During the next week, pay attention to your feelings. When you are aware that you are experiencing a feeling, take a moment to reflect on these questions:

- What is this feeling that I am feeling? What name would I give it? What are the thoughts that are associated with the feeling, that are behind the feeling?
- To what extent are these thoughts based on objective evidence? To what extent are they realistic? To what extent are there grounds for these thoughts? To what extent are they distortions?
- What are some alternative thoughts I could have about this, thoughts which are perhaps more objective and based on evidence?
- If they are, to some extent, distorted, where does this distortion come from? What are its origins?
- What is the function of this distortion? How do I use it?
- How should I react to these thoughts? What, if anything, should I do with them?

Remember that there is always a reason for irrational and distorted thinking. There is always some inner logic to it that may not make sense to anyone else in the world but makes sense to us. Somehow it is functional—at least in the short run and in our own brains. When you become irrational and distorted in your thinking, it is useful to ask yourself where it comes from, what function it is performing for you and how you use it. This is one good way of learning more about yourself, what makes you tick. It is a very good way of getting in touch with what you are afraid of, what you are avoiding and how you may be overprotecting yourself in ways that are keeping you from loving and working the way you want to.

In fact, becoming aware of irrational and distorted thinking is often all you have to do to manage those thoughts so that they don't become a problem. Awareness is a very useful and much underrated tool for building a good life, because once we are aware of what we are doing, thinking or feeling, we can manage it so that it works for us.

I once attended a five-day personal growth program. On the first day, there was a sign on the wall with letters so small they were hard to read. Each day, the letters in the sign became bigger until, on the final day, you couldn't miss them. The sign said: WHAT AM I PRETENDING NOT TO KNOW?

In other words, what am I being dense about? How am I using that denseness to protect myself and avoid dealing with things I need to deal with? What am I keeping myself from knowing as a way of staying safe and avoiding stress and pain? It's a wonderful question that we should all ask ourselves at least once a week.

A note of caution: It doesn't make sense to blame or berate yourself for creating irrational and distorted thoughts or pretending not to know things that you should know. That behavior didn't come out of nowhere. It's not random. You were not born with it. Those thoughts grew in you while you were growing up. You came to believe them because of the experiences you had as an infant, child, adolescent and adult. You use them to justify yourself, avoid pain and protect yourself. What's wrong with that? It's not that they are bad; they just don't work very well.

Chapter 12

GETTING TO KNOW
THE STRANGER INSIDE

One of the hardest things about being alive is knowing that our behavior is, to some extent, controlled by deep, inner forces of which we are not aware. This is part of the dark side, because it influences our behavior, but unless we learn to manage it, it operates outside of our control.

How can we learn to manage this part of ourselves so that it doesn't create problems? How can we use its positive aspects to live more the way we want to live?

Sigmund Freud is credited with the discovery of the unconscious as a psychic force. As a keen observer of human behavior and a naturalist of the human mind, he was struck by the fact that people made errors—of speech, of hearing, of forgetting, of missing appointments, of losing things—and that there was a pattern to the errors. The errors were not random. There was a meaning behind them. From this, he inferred that there must be some force below the level of awareness that was driving this behavior. In retrospect, this should not be surprising to us. There is much material in our minds which is below the surface of consciousness but which we can bring up to the surface easily. If you want to experience this for yourself you can do this demonstration:

In your mind's eye, bring up the image of the house in which you lived when you were seven or eight years old. Imagine yourself walking around the house and seeing the various rooms and what was in them. If you're having trouble bringing up the image of the house you lived in as a child, bring up the image of any house you have lived in previously.

This is proof that there are images, memories, thoughts and beliefs in your mind of which you are not consciously aware. Our minds contain billions of bytes of information, memories, images and thoughts. It's a good thing that we're not aware of all of them at the same time. If we were, our minds would be a constant jumble. Happily, we have the ability to manipulate and manage all of this data so that it serves us and helps us to do what we want to do and live the way we want to live. We can bring some of it into our consciousness when we need it and let it recede below the surface when we don't.

But what if there is a part of our minds that drives our behavior, our emotions and our thinking and of which we are never or seldom aware? What if there is a part of our minds that is so deep, scary, uncomfortable or shameful that we don't want to be aware of it? For the great majority of us that is, in fact, the case. There is a part of our minds that is deep and hidden and which sometimes drives our behavior.

Psychotherapists have given this part of the mind many different names. Some call it the unconscious, others call it deep structure, core material or schema. Most would agree that it is made up of beliefs, feelings, assumptions, attitudes and habits of thinking and feeling that have been growing in us since we were born.

First step: Awareness

Here are examples of some of the beliefs, assumptions and habits of thought that lurk below the surface of consciousness and cause problems for people:

- No matter what I do or how hard I try, things will never work out.
- The best way for me to survive is to hunker down and wait things out.

- Even though I have been somewhat successful, if people really knew about me, I'd be in big trouble.
- Whenever I win, I lose.
- If I outdo my father (or mother), he'll be angry with me and there will be hell to pay.
- No matter how much I try to hide it, deep down I'm not very loveable.
- It's just not okay for me to go with the flow, take things as they come and just enjoy life.
- If I allow myself to express my anger, somebody (maybe me) is going to get hurt.
- I can't depend on other people. I have to do it by myself.
- If I'm not careful, other people will take advantage of me.
- If I just keep going, keep my head down and don't look up, things will work out.
- The one thing I don't want (but I need to keep it a secret—from myself as well as others) is for other people to depend on me.
- If I can just keep attracting women (or men), I won't have to grow up and be responsible.
- It's really not okay for me to have fun and enjoy myself.
- Since I'm really unlikable and unworthy, in order to make it in this world I'm going to have to fool people.
- Maybe if I appear weak and helpless enough, some good soul will save my life.
- In order to survive, I'm going to have to be better than other people.
- If I'm not very successful and outstanding, I don't deserve to be here.

Awareness of these deep, hidden beliefs, assumptions and habits of thought and feeling is the key, because once people become aware of these forces, they can manage them.

This core material or unconscious mind is not all bad or hurtful. As we will see, it can be very helpful and affirming. Still, the idea that there is a part of our minds that can drive our behavior but of which we are not aware is scary. It means that some of what we do or don't do is done or not done for reasons we are not aware of and over which we have no control. What can we do to become more aware of these forces so that we can at least know about them and gain *some* control over them?

Total accountability: Stop, look and listen

There are some things you can do to become aware of your unconscious. They are relatively simple but they take some work as well as courage and conviction.

The simplest thing you can do is pay attention to what you do and what happens to you, not to what you think you wanted to do or wanted to happen to you, and ask yourself:

- How did I contribute to doing this or to this happening?
- Why might I have wanted to do that? Why might I have wanted that to happen?
- What does this tell me about what is going on inside of me that I may not be aware of?

This is especially helpful when what you have done or what has happened to you is not what you wanted to have happen; when it is, in fact, something that will cause pain, problems, hardship or unwanted complications.

Here is an exercise you can use to get some practice in total accountability:

Accountability Dyad Exercise

Find another person with whom to do this exercise and a safe, quiet place in which to do it.

1. Person A tells Person B about a time when something happened to him that he didn't want to happen and which was painful and damaging.

2. Person B asks Person A three questions:
   - How did you contribute to that happening?
   - Why might you have wanted that to happen?
   - What does this tell you about some of the drives, beliefs and attitudes that are hidden deep in your unconscious but are nevertheless driving your behavior?
3. Person A does his best to answer the questions, not worrying about whether his answer is on the mark or not.
4. Exchange roles and repeat the exercise.

Dreams and awareness

There is another way to uncover what is going on beneath the surface of consciousness. It involves learning from our dreams.

Dreams are one avenue into deep, hidden parts of ourselves. After all, dreams are the images we create while our conscious minds are out of the picture. While we are sleeping, the filtering and censoring functions of our conscious minds are dormant. So the deeper, more essential material can come up and present itself for consideration. Sigmund Freud referred to dreams as the royal road to the unconscious.

The first step in using dreams is to remember them. One way of doing that is to tell yourself before you go to sleep that you are going to remember your dream and to put a notebook and pen on your bedside table. As soon as you wake up—even before you are fully conscious—write down whatever you remember of your dream. You may recall only brief snatches or a few disjointed images. Write them down. Even fragments of dreams can be useful. You can use this next exercise to get some idea about what the dream is telling you.

Learning From Your Dreams

There are hundreds (perhaps thousands) of approaches to interpreting dreams. The one I like is a Jungian approach which I learned through reading Robert Johnson's book *Inner Work:*

Step One: Associations
Make a list of all your dream images and write your associations (words, ideas, memories and feelings) for each image. Spend some time reflecting on these associations.

Step Two: Dynamics
Addressing each dream image individually, identify and connect your dream images to parts of yourself, certain personality traits or behaviors and functions in your life. Write down your examples connecting your dream images to specific dynamics in your inner life.

Step Three: Interpretations
Combine your work from the first two steps and craft a coherent statement of what the dream means to you as whole. Reflect on the dream's message, advice, meaning for your life and insight.

Step Four: Rituals
Integrate your interpretation into your waking life and apply a physical act to your life that will affirm the dream's message. The act can be practical or symbolic.[1]

Some of my clients have been helped significantly by their dreams. Timon came to me suffering from horrible physical ailments for which doctors could find no explanation. He often became so weak that he couldn't stand up for hours at a time. He experienced excruciatingly painful headaches that made him dizzy and see double. He had back problems and arthritic knees. Timon told me about a dream in which he was the captain of an army unit that had been attacked and surrounded by a wall that was closing in on him. The unit pulled off a miraculous escape at the last minute. Once free, he started berating his men, calling them stupid and cowardly, and he single-handedly took on the job of attacking the enemy.

As we worked at understanding the dream, Timon came to see that there was a tremendous amount of rage inside of him that he wasn't acknowledging or expressing. He had been abused and abandoned as a child and had many reasons to be enraged. He also was very critical of himself but, instead of knowing that, tried to come across as perfect, brilliant and strong and to put tremendous effort into performing heroically. Twice before in his life he had worked very hard and become very successful and then lost it all. Unable to perform as heroically as he wanted to, he was extremely disappointed with himself. Instead of knowing that and suffering the pain of that knowledge, he was very critical of other people, especially his wife. Shortly after becoming aware of these dynamics through the dream, he experienced a spontaneous remission and regained his ability to perform his responsibilities as a husband and father. The dream helped Timon to become aware of the rage inside of him, to see it as understandable and to become more comfortable with it. It also helped him see how he had put so much pressure on himself that it was impossible for him to meet his own expectations. Avoiding the shame of not meeting those expectations, he was brutally critical of others. Through the dream, he became more comfortable with his imperfections and less hard on himself. He could feel bad about not being the hero he wanted to be and stop being so critical of other people.

Joy came to me complaining that whenever she was around people she didn't know, she became very anxious and suffered from panic attacks, often having to leave abruptly and confining herself to her house. We did some work in which I taught her some relaxation techniques and she imagined herself in increasingly scary situations while using the relaxation techniques to stay calm. She then began to allow herself to be around strangers and to force herself to remain there even when she felt uncomfortable. Slowly, she became more able to be in such situations without becoming anxious and panicky.

Then Joy had a series of dreams in which she was riding in the back of a convertible, having a wonderful time. Sometimes she was holding a baby with her. In her dreams, all of a sudden a blanket came over her or the baby was somehow taken from her and her fun was abruptly extinguished. She learned from the dreams that there was a part of her that longed to live a more carefree and adventurous life, to express the child part of her that had been short-changed and cut off. She had always been very responsible, focused on taking care of other people—including two husbands and several relatives—and doing what was "right" and what she was supposed to do. She didn't pay any attention to the part of her that wanted to take off, go wherever and enjoy life. We worked on helping her find a middle ground in which she could begin to honor that part of herself that had been so ignored and discounted.

Joy began to become more comfortable in all kinds of social situations and more willing to do things that she wanted to do even if other people didn't understand it or approve of it. Three months after leaving therapy, I saw her in a parking lot. She was driving a sports car and beginning to honor that younger, fun-loving part of herself without abandoning her responsibilities to her family.

I have gained some valuable insights from my dreams. About two years ago I had a dream in which a real estate agent I know was presenting a training program. I was having a hard time understanding; I was looking at papers and outlines but just not getting it. At some point I looked up and saw another man I know sitting on the real estate agent's knee and being very chummy with him. That made me very jealous. Finally, I noticed the other man carefully putting a document into a file and I decided I'd better do that too. In thinking about what this dream might be telling me, I realized that both of these men are very personable and pleasant men and also very shrewd and calculating. What I took the dream to be telling me was that I wanted to be more like them. I wanted to be more strategic, to get better at finding the balance between being "a nice guy" and also being shrewd and calculating and getting what I wanted. The dream also told me that I was skeptical of that kind of shrewdness and wanted to be careful it didn't turn me into too much of a "smooth operator," too manipulative and strategic.

I have a recurring dream in which I can't locate my wallet or briefcase and am very upset about it but then find that I am able to do whatever I wanted to do without the wallet or briefcase. The message to me has been that I don't have to be so concerned about being orderly and careful and organized, that I can trust myself to have inside of me whatever I need to get the things done that I want to get done or to live the way I want to live.

In another recurring dream, I am with a large group of people that is divided into smaller groups and cliques. I am not happy with the group of which I am a part. I want to be in a group that is more prestigious, sophisticated, successful, good-looking, popular, wealthy and exalted. But I don't make any attempt to join that more exalted group out of fear that they will reject me. So I end up being with nobody and am very dissatisfied and uncomfortable. I take this dream to be a wake-up call to me, a message that if I always want to be somewhere I'm not, I'm going to be perpetually disappointed and dissatisfied and that I'm going to be a lot happier if I can be fully and presently wherever I am. I have also learned from the dream that it is okay for me to have an extreme need for friends and approval from others and to work at getting that. I don't like that about myself. I wish it weren't true, but it is true so I can accept it and live with it.

Remember Friedrich Perl's insight that the first step in changing yourself is surrendering to what is really true right now, accepting it, even loving it. If we keep on resisting it and fighting it, we use up a lot of energy and get stuck.

I encourage all of you to take your dreams seriously and to make an attempt to let them tell you some things that will be helpful to you in living the way you want to live.

There are no accidents

Another relatively simple way of getting in touch with your unconscious dynamics is to pay attention to the errors that you make—errors of hearing, speaking, forgetting, losing things, missing appointments—and work at making some sense out of them, perhaps finding a pattern in them, some meaning from them.

In the process of telling me a story, a colleague of mine said "my second wife," which was a slip since he was in his first marriage. The slip doesn't mean that he is going to have a second wife, but it certainly suggests that something might be going on inside that he might want to examine. Forgetting is a common way for unconscious dynamics to play themselves out. As I say to people who have a hard time owning the significance of their forgetting: "Funny thing, I've never forgotten a date with a woman whom I cared about or a date to play tennis or golf."

Here is an example of a mistake I made that I didn't pay attention to at my peril. Several years ago, I went to work as a psychotherapist for a community mental health center north of Denver. I worked part-time at the center and part-time at a nearby community health clinic. It wasn't a good situation. The director of the center and I had very different ideas regarding what mental illness entailed and how to treat it. During this time, I traveled to southern New Mexico every two or three weeks to spend a weekend with my wife. On one of my trips back to Denver, I took my keys out my pocket to go through the security checkpoint at the airport and failed to reclaim them at the other side of the checkpoint. Just prior to getting on the plane, I realized I didn't have my keys, which included the one to my car that was parked at the airport in Denver. I quickly ran to the airport police station to see if anyone had turned in my keys. Not finding them, I got on the plane and had a colleague pick me up at the airport and take me to my apartment to retrieve another key. It was a big hassle.

Later that same week, I locked my key to the office inside my apartment without a way to get back into the apartment and had to get the apartment manager to let me in. About a week later, the director fired me.

I believe "forgetting" those keys were no accidents. I had been through that security checkpoint many times before without leaving my keys behind. When I went back to retrieve my keys, instead of going to the security checkpoint, which is where they probably were, I went to the airport police station, which is where they weren't. In fact, upon my return to the El Paso airport, I retrieved the keys that I had left at the checkpoint.

Upon getting fired, I relived those "forgetting" experiences to make sense out of them. Apparently I had picked up some cues from the director that he was going to fire me. He knew that he was going to do that at least a couple of weeks before he did it. Somewhere inside of me, below my level of consciousness, I knew that I was in trouble. For some reason, I didn't want to go to work. Something was wrong. Had I paid attention to this "forgetting," I doubt that it would have saved my job, but it would have enabled me to take some corrective action that might have made my recovery easier than it turned out to be.

If you want to get some glimpses into what is going on deep inside, below the level of your consciousness, take your errors seriously. Look for meaning in them; ask them what they have to teach you.

One example of this is people who are chronically late. Most of us know somebody who is always a little late and always has an excuse. This is a case of unconscious dynamics playing themselves out. Such people are, I believe, being driven by some of these forces:

- They want you to know they are more important than you. Their time is more valuable than yours.
- They want you to know they are special. They don't have to follow the rules.
- They want you to know that they are very busy.
- They want to be noticed, to make an entrance.
- They don't want to be there.

I don't think these people are consciously late for these reasons. But I do believe there is a powerful dynamic of which they are unaware that drives them to be late. In order to change this pattern of behavior, they would have to take a good look at it and ask themselves: *What is going on here? Why might I want to be doing this? What is the payoff from this behavior?*

This is also true of "accidents." Most accidents are preventable. They are often a result of not paying attention and they may sometimes be caused by unconscious dynamics. Shortly after I began a new job, one of the more experienced workers was showing me how to do something on the computer. As I was listening to him, I was thinking, *What a bunch of BS. It's ridiculous that we have to do this. The whole world is being taken over by computers.* Somehow or other my knee found a way to bump the computer's power button, abruptly cutting off the training session. I don't believe that I consciously turned off the computer with my knee. But I do believe that somewhere inside of me there was an intention—unconscious though it might have been—to shut the computer down.

There are also some more exotic ways of getting in touch with that hidden part of yourself. One of them is called active imagination. It was developed by psychiatrist Carl Jung and involves having a conversation with an imaginary being you bring into your mind while in a waking, relaxed state. The basic method is to find a quiet place, put yourself into a relaxed state through some kind of relaxation ritual, call up the image of some wise, perhaps magical, being with whom you would like to relate, ask him or her what he or she has to say, open up to him or her and listen to him or her. Write down the dialogue that you have with the wise being. This technique is well described in Robert Johnson's book *Inner Work.*

Here are three simple exercises you can do to get in touch with your unconscious thoughts, feelings and motivations:

Admitting Accountability

Whenever anything happens to you that you didn't think you wanted to have happen or whenever you do something which you didn't think you wanted to do, ask yourself:

- How did I contribute to that happening?
- Why might I have wanted that to happen or why might I have done that?

- What can this tell me about some of the deep-seated beliefs, assumptions, attitudes and habits that are driving my behavior?

Attending to Errors and Accidents

Pay close attention to the errors that you make—errors of speech, hearing and forgetting—as well as any accidents that occur. Ask yourself:

- If I assumed that there was some meaning to these errors, that there is some significant message behind them, what would they be telling me?
- What can I learn from these mistakes?

Learning From Your Dreams

Use the technique described in this chapter (or some other technique which you like better) to interpret your dreams and find out what they are telling you.

Be careful about how you defend yourself

Earlier, I discussed the value of emotional pain and discomfort. One of the things that makes it hard to live well is that the most valuable tool we have can sometimes bring pain and discomfort. Naturally, we try to defend ourselves against that pain and discomfort. Much of that defense goes on below the level of consciousness and results in behavior that isn't under our conscious control. Again, the best we can do is become aware of these unconscious dynamics so that we can manage them to some extent.

When I first heard of defense mechanisms, I was a college student in the process of knowing everything and I was so heavily defended that I decided there was no way I could be afflicted with such irrationality. Now, I know that we all find ways of defending ourselves against emotional pain, unwanted thoughts and unacceptable impulses. It's not a question of whether we use defense mechanisms or not; it's a question of *how* we use them. If life becomes so scary and intolerable that we can't stand it, we can create our own reality (delusion). Instead of owning and accepting the fact that we are angry with somebody, we make believe that the person is angry with us (projection). Instead of owning our own sexual desire and the difficulty of expressing it, we project it onto society and get involved in anti-pornography campaigns (reaction formation). Instead of accepting and expressing our aggression toward the boss, we take it out on our spouse or our children or the dog (displacement). Instead of using our anger and aggression to kill and maim the perpetrators of racial segregation, we use it to fuel a non-violent civil rights campaign that wins victory without bloodshed (sublimation).

Some defense mechanisms throw people into psychosis. Others make life difficult and get in the way of interpersonal relationships. Still others enable us to live well. Here is a list of some of the most common ones and examples of how they are applied. They are listed roughly in order of the degree to which they cause problems for people, ranging from psychotic defenses to relatively benign ones:

- **Denial:** Refusing to acknowledge reality, believing something is true which is obviously not true. Example: Believing that someone who is dead is still alive. Believing that one still has a job which one no longer has.
- **Delusion/Distortion:** Believing that something is true without credible evidence that it is. Example: Believing that people are talking about you without evidence that they are. Believing that you are more skilled, powerful or capable than the evidence supports. Believing that, because you are so important, the CIA has implanted a device in you and is monitoring your thoughts.
- **Schizoid Fantasy:** Using daydreaming and fantasy to avoid discomfort and conflict and to make oneself feel better,

especially as a way of cutting oneself off from other people. Example: Fantasizing about what you're going to say to somebody or how you're going to resolve a conflict or how you're going to win somebody over, instead of actually doing it.

- **Projection:** Dealing with uncomfortable and unwanted feelings by imagining that they are held by other people. Example: Instead of being aware of your own anger, imagining that other people are angry. Avoiding awareness of your own imperfection by focusing on the imperfections of others.

- **Acting Out:** Avoiding the uncomfortable feeling of a difficult wish or impulse by directly expressing it. Example: Blowing up in a temper tantrum or using drugs or alcohol to relieve tension.

- **Passive-Aggressive Behavior:** Hurting other people in indirect ways that can't be easily challenged. Example: Being chronically late and "forgetting" things in ways that hurt other people.

- **Repression:** A milder form of denial consisting of inexplicable naiveté, not seeing things that everyone else sees. Example: Not realizing you're in trouble at work when everyone else does. Not realizing your marriage is in trouble until your spouse says he or she is leaving.

- **Displacement:** The redirection of feelings toward a relatively less cared for person instead of the person or situation arousing the feelings. Example: Taking one's frustration out on the family rather than on the boss.

- **Reaction Formation:** Behaving in a way exactly the opposite of an unacceptable, instinctual impulse. Example: Making believe you love someone whom you actually hate. Caring for someone else when you actually want to be cared for.

- **Dissociation:** Changing one's state of being to avoid emotional pain. Example: "Going off" into a foggy state, not being "all there," out-of-body experiences, hysterical reactions and making believe things are not as serious as they are or that one is different from how one really is.

- **Intellectualization:** Focusing on ideas instead of feelings, things instead of people, irrelevant details instead of relationships. Example: Getting involved in arguments about who is right or wrong when the real issue is concern over the strength and durability of an emotional bond.

The important point is that we all use some of these defenses. They are not necessarily harmful. The same bizarre or impulsive behavior may be harmful and dysfunctional dissociation in one case and creative, fulfilling artistic expression in another. Whether it is one or the other depends on the reasons for it, the motivation behind it and the impact it has on your ability to live the way you want to live.

Often, defense mechanisms are helpful to us. Denial, for example, is a perfectly normal and functional response to the threat of severe loss—diagnosis of a life-threatening disease, for example— as long as it doesn't go on for too long a time. That is the point. Defense mechanisms can be helpful or harmful, depending on how they are used and their impact on us. Only we know the difference and only we can manage them effectively. In fact, certain defense mechanisms are associated with healthy living. In his insightful report from a study of a graduating class at Harvard (*Adaptation to Life*), George Vaillant describes five defense mechanisms that were used by the most successful and healthiest men in the study:

- **Altruism:** Using one's energy and talent to help others.
- **Sublimation:** Converting the energy from anger and aggressiveness into creative activity.

- **Suppression:** Acknowledging a painful conflict or problem and deciding to put off dealing with it until a later time.

- **Anticipation:** Planning for future inner discomfort. For example, setting up a support system to help one deal with a problem that one knows one has to face.

- **Humor:** Expression of ideas or feelings without unpleasant effects on others.[2]

How can you become aware of the defense mechanisms that you are using so that you can manage them more effectively? You can use admitting accountability, attention to errors and accidents and learning from dreams to become more aware of what is going on inside, beneath the level of consciousness. Awareness is the essential first step. Once you are aware of what you are doing and the forces that are driving it, you can begin to manage it. In fact, you will automatically do that.

A final thought about the unconscious: because it is scary to realize that much of what we do or don't do is driven by forces of which we are not aware, we tend to regard unconscious dynamics as negative, dark, foreboding and dangerous. But our unconscious is also the source of inspiration, insight and intuition. It can be a wonderfully creative and affirming force. If we allow it to, it can help us make good decisions for ourselves, seize opportunities and choose the right path.

Chapter 13

GETTING ALONG WITHOUT GIVING UP TOO MUCH OF YOURSELF

The virtue of selfishness

We have been told that it is not good to be selfish, that we should be generous and loving and concerned about other people. We have also been told that we won't be able to love other people unless we love ourselves and that if we don't take care of ourselves, we won't be able to take care of anyone else. How do we reconcile these competing messages?

We must acknowledge that we are born with powerful drives to survive and thrive. If our ability to survive and thrive is threatened, we can become ferocious. Once, I was giving a talk on anger to a group of middle-aged women. When I told them that human beings are ferocious animals, they looked at me with doubt and wonder. Then I said: "Just imagine someone messing around with one of your children and you'll see what I mean." They understood. It is this ferociousness that gives a dark complexion to human relationships.

We are born with powerful drives to use our bodies, minds, spirits and emotions to do what we want to do, eat what we want to eat and sleep where we want to sleep. Fortunately, we are also driven by a desire to love whom we want to love in the way we want to love them and to express ourselves in the way we want to express ourselves. This combination of powerful drives to use our abilities in expressing ourselves and to love whom and how we want to love makes it possible that, in the process of satisfying those drives, we are going to help other people. In a way, the more selfish we are, the more helpful we are likely to be.

This isn't always the case. If it were, we wouldn't be troubled by all the violence and hurt in the world. What gets in the way of this positive dynamic? When the ability of people to satisfy these drives is threatened, they lash out and attack. When people have been traumatized and terrorized, they become angry and afraid and use their abilities to hurt other people. When people are taught that they shouldn't be selfish, that they should always act in the interests of others and not serve themselves, that they should never be angry, jealous or hateful, they eventually hurt themselves or others.

What can we do as individuals to keep this dynamic between selfishness and the welfare of others going in the right direction? First, we can acknowledge and honor our powerful drives to survive and thrive. When we repress those drives, they come out in uncontrollable and hurtful ways. Second, we can become aware of anything which threatens our ability to satisfy those drives and quickly take creative action to mitigate it without unduly hurting other people. Third, we can use our abilities to keep other people from being so traumatized and threatened that they lash out.

Let's look at some creative ways of acknowledging, experiencing and using our selfishness.

We live with other people. We are social animals. We live in families. Our economic system has evolved over thousands of years into one which is based on interdependence and interchange. Much of our joy and suffering is based in relationships with others. It's virtually impossible to live well without being able to get along with others. But, precisely because other people are so important to us, we have to be careful that we don't let our concern for others and our desire to get along with them lead us to compromise ourselves excessively, give up too much of ourselves.

If we do that we face a real dilemma: We either live inauthentic, constricted lives or we become resentful, mean and hard to get along with. It's another example of the pay-me-now-or-pay-me-later phenomenon. If I let you take advantage of me, excessively constrain me or harm me in any significant way without doing anything about it, we will live in harmony only in the short run. In the long run, we will be living in a pitched battle, fighting trench warfare, a war of attrition in which we both lose.

Do sweat the small stuff and learn to fight fairly over it

When George Bach, a marriage and family therapist, first started practice, married couples came in complaining about fighting too much and he tried to get them to stop fighting. He then did some research on his own. He got the names of fifty "happily married" couples from friends and interviewed them all in depth. On the basis of the interviews he determined that only three of the couples were really happily married. The most significant distinguishing characteristic of those couples was that they were constantly fighting. But their fights were different from the typical fights of married couples in three ways: First, they were always fighting about the real issues. Second, they never tried to hurt each other during the fights by bringing up past grievances, calling each other names or attacking each other. Third, they never let grievances build up. When one had a problem with the other's behavior, they addressed it immediately and dealt with it instead of letting the little grievances build up until they were big and hard to manage.

So Bach changed his practice dramatically. He started teaching couples how to fight—but how to fight fairly—in ways that addressed grievances quickly (even the little, petty ones), didn't hurt either of the partners and didn't let the little things build up into big ones.

If you're married, you're familiar with this problem: Your spouse does something that bugs you. But it's a little thing. He puts the small jars in the part of the refrigerator that's reserved for the tall bottles, thereby leaving no room for the tall bottles. She snaps at you in front of your friends or puts you down in subtle ways at a party. You ask him to do some small favor for you and he doesn't do it, "forgets," as it were. He "forgets" to give you phone messages. You say to yourself, *I'm not going to bug him or her about that. I don't want to be petty. It's not such a big thing. I can live with it.* But the little issues build up and, before you know it, you are deeply resentful, seething inside, not wanting to touch him or her. You don't want to make love, so that also becomes an issue. Things are deteriorating and you're in a mess.

One way of dealing with this is to tell yourself, *I'm just going to have to accept these little inconveniences and petty grievances caused by _____'s thoughtlessness, forgetfulness and stubbornness. They're not that important. I can live with them.* But that may be a big mistake. Because those acts of inconsiderateness and forgetfulness may actually reflect deeper, more important issues that are real threats to your relationship and need to be addressed. Those deeper issues may be real threats to the emotional bond on which love relationships are based. Remember what we learned about the significance of little errors as windows into the unconscious.

When Nancy and I fell in love and decided to get married, the tacit, unspoken agreement was that she would take care of me, the spacey genius—keep me from walking into walls and give me the unconditional love and support that I wouldn't give myself— and I would give her an entree into the world of adventure, enterprise and risk, something she wouldn't do for herself.

During the early years of our marriage one of the patterns of our relationship was that whenever we left the house, Nancy checked me over: "Did you remember to do this or that?" "Have you made sure about that or this?" At some point I began to resent the questions—partly because I was growing up and didn't find the mother-son aspects of our relationship to be very satisfying. There followed a couple of years of constant fighting over this issue until Nancy slowly stopped taking care of me in that way—partly because she could see that I was doing a better job of taking care of myself. The point is that in order to make that change, I had to protest every time she switched to the caretaker routine, until we both got so sick of it that we changed. The other point is that the reason it was so important to address this petty issue was that it was threatening the emotional bond of love between us.

The first principle of getting along with others without giving up too much of yourself is: *Do* sweat the small stuff—and do something about it. There are two reasons for this:

- The small stuff may well be a reflection of deeper, larger issues that will threaten the emotional bonds of your relationship.
- If you don't address it, the small stuff can eventually build up into big stuff.

Before we get into how to address the small stuff, realize that the way you know the behavior of somebody else is bothering you is that you feel it. You feel it in your stomach, your head, your bones, your legs and arms or wherever else fear, anger and resentment is expressed in your particular body/mind.

Assertiveness: Once more, lightly

What do you do when your perception of somebody else's behavior—what somebody else is doing or not doing—is creating feelings of anxiety, anger, resentment or fear in you? You tell the person what is going on with you in a way that is not likely to make them defensive. You use certain principles of non-defensive communication that are succinctly described in an article by psychologist Jack Gibb:[1]

- **Describe, don't evaluate.** The most effective opening you can make in this conversation of confrontation is to start with "I" and tell the other person what you are seeing, hearing and/or feeling. Describe what you are perceiving without making any judgments or evaluations of it.

- **Talk in terms of having a problem, not having a solution.** Describe how the behavior of the other person is a problem for you. Don't suggest that you know what to do about it, that you have a solution. Invite the other person to join with you in exploring possible approaches to resolution.
- **Don't be strategic or manipulative.** As you are describing what is going on with you and your view of the problem, be straightforward and direct. Don't beat around the bush. Don't mince words. Don't put it off on the other person by saying something like "How would you feel if…"
- **Be empathetic, not cold and neutral.** Let the other person know that you realize that there are other things in his or her life besides worrying about how his or her behavior is affecting you—that there may be plenty of reasons for the behavior that is at issue.
- **Speak as an equal, not as a superior.** This is a good idea even if you are in a position of authority over the other person.
- **Be provisional, not certain.** Let the other person know that you are open to hearing his or her response, that you're bringing this matter up in order to explore it, address it and confront it, not to impose a solution that you have already decided upon.

This conversation is not going to be as clean or orderly as suggested by these steps. But as you have the conversation, keep the steps in mind and use them as a guide.

We have been working on what to do when the behavior of somebody else creates a problem for you. What about the opposite situation? Somebody comes to you and tells you that your behavior is creating a problem for him or her. This may well happen to readers of this book who are working at changing themselves and the way in which they live. The people who live with such readers or are close to them will be just as affected by the changes as the readers themselves.

Dr. Thomas Gordon has written a number of books that contain useful responses to people who say they are having problems with your behavior. His first and most popular book was called *Parent Effectiveness Training*. He wrote it to help the parents of teenagers avoid the power struggles that arise in those years without abandoning their responsibilities as parents. Here is the approach that he suggests, again to be regarded as principles rather than a script for a conversation.[2]

- **Let the other person know you heard what s/he said and that you would like to hear more.** This is what Dr. Gordon calls "active listening." The best way to let the other person know you heard what s/he said is to repeat it back to him or her as you heard it and to check if you heard it right. This is very disarming. It will calm the other person down, encourage him or her to say more and set the stage for useful confrontation. Important distinction: You are not saying that you agree with what the other person said—just that you heard it.

- **Ask open-ended questions for clarification.** Open-ended questions are questions that don't have "Yes" or "No" answers and that invite the other person to think, reason and express him or herself. Ask questions such as: What is it about what I did or didn't do that bothers you? Can you give me some examples of when I've done that or when that has happened?

- **Give the other person your response to what you have heard.** Now that you have worked at understanding the situation, get in touch with your response to it and share it with the other person. As much as possible, use simple, straightforward and direct language.

- **Invite the other person to join you in exploring approaches to solving the problem.**

These techniques can be useful in all of life's contexts: in romantic relationships, in parent-child relationships, in the workplace, with friends and with family.

The creative use of conflict

In a way, what we're talking about is how to use conflict to make things better. I once worked for an organization which placed a very high value on acknowledging and addressing conflict quickly and openly. I heard the executive vice president tell his senior management team something which has stuck with me: "If you have a problem with me," he said, "the most loyal thing you can do is come to me and tell me about it. The most disloyal thing you can do is tell somebody else about it." That value was infused into the organization through a series of training sessions on the Pinch Model. Employees were taught what to do when they had a "pinch" (a visceral, uncomfortable feeling in the stomach, head or some other part of the body) with another employee. They were taught how to address the "pinch" with the other person in a way that didn't make the other person defensive and how to respond when others relayed "pinch" messages to them. There was less backbiting, gossip and underhanded conflict in that organization than in any of which I have been a part.

Active listening is so valuable that I'm going to decribe it again. If you use this simple technique it will make a big difference in your relationships with other people.

When anybody comes to you and says in any way that s/he is having a problem with your behavior or lack of behavior, you let the person know you heard what s/he said by reflecting it back to him or her. You check to see if you've heard the person correctly and you encourage the person to say more about it by asking open-ended questions designed to give you more information about how your behavior is affecting the person. One great question is: "Can you give me an example?" Only after you have taken these first two steps do you give the person your reaction to what s/he has said.

One more illustration from my life: When my son was young, he became angry at me for good reasons (for example, not letting him do what he wanted to do) and he said: "I hate you, Dad. You're the worst father in the world." I replied, "I hear you saying that you hate me and that I'm the worst father in the world." If I'd been a little smarter back then I would have asked him: "What am I doing or not doing that is making you hate me?" But just letting him know that I heard him say he hated me was very powerful. It let him know that he could tell me that and assured him that it was okay to hate me, that hating me was a very understandable and natural reaction to not being permitted to do everything he wanted to do. It allowed him to become more comfortable with what was going on inside him and made it possible for us to do some negotiating in our relationship.

Love: Relationships that force us to grow

Love relationships are a special case. Aside from being extremely pleasurable and even numinous, they are a wonderful medium for learning about ourselves and striving toward psychological health. As we all know, romantic love can also be fraught with pain and suffering. In his book *Care of the Soul*, Thomas Moore has a chapter entitled "Love's Initiations." In it he writes about how we talk about love lightly without acknowledging how powerful and lasting it can be. We expect love to be healing and whole and are surprised when it creates hollow gaps and empty failures. But it is so powerful and self-renewing that even after we have been hurt by it, we enter freely into it once again, knowing that whenever we fall in love, we are vulnerable.[3]

One of the reasons love relationships are so complicated is that we fall in love with people for reasons that are deeper than we think. In one fascinating piece of research, women were given the dirty T-shirts of men and asked to pick the ones that smelled good. It turned out that women were attracted to the T-shirts of men with whom, if they mated, their offspring would have strong immune systems. Apparently there was something primordial and biologically hardwired going on.[4]

There is also evidence that we fall in love with people who have characteristics that we covet and who have qualities of our mothers and/or fathers. This makes sense. None of us is whole.

We all live with certain gaps in our personalities, deficiencies that we would like to correct. Falling in love with somebody who has characteristics we value but don't possess seems like a relatively easy way of filling the gap.

But why would we fall in love with people who are similar to our mothers and/or fathers? Several good reasons come to mind: First, since we are familiar with our mothers and fathers, it might seem safe to fall in love with someone like them. Second, if we didn't receive all of the affirmation, love and support that we wanted from our mothers and fathers (as few of us do), we might fall in love with someone like them in order to correct that deficiency. Third, if there are wounds that we would like to heal with our mothers and fathers, it makes sense to fall in love with someone like them as a surrogate with whom it may be easier to heal such wounds.

My wife Nancy has a lot of common sense. She also has a way of staying calm in difficult situations and being able to act effectively even when under lots of stress. Those are two qualities I wanted but lacked. She also was able to give me the support that I wouldn't give myself. She's a lot like my mother. Both are social workers. Both are introverted. Both are unaware of how good they are and have a higher need for external support than is warranted.

I, on the other hand, am very extroverted and am willing to put myself into social situations in which I am a stranger. I have a relatively high tolerance for stressful situations and I enjoy being with other people "out in the world." I'm a good talker and can be superficially friendly with many people. I can be charming and I place much importance on impressing other people. I can also be very self-absorbed and imperious (easily hurt by criticism) in a way that isn't obvious to people who don't know me well. These were all characteristics of Nancy's father.

Often, we fall in love with people for reasons of which we are unaware but which make much sense. However, over time these qualities can begin to cause problems. Using the other person's characteristics as a way of filling personal deficiencies begins to wear thin. We begin to resent the qualities that we once coveted. We find ourselves wanting to develop those characteristics ourselves. We find that our partners are not helping us to heal the wounds that we need to heal with our mothers and fathers and resentment begins to build. If this pattern continues unheeded and unaddressed, it can lead to breach and divorce.

If, on the other hand, the pattern is exposed and comes to light and both of the partners are willing and able to withstand the discomfort of self-awareness, they can help each other to grow and heal, but only if each of the partners is willing to change. In order to help each other, both partners have to accept their imperfections and work at changing. My belief is that these dynamics bring most marriages to a crisis point at which one of three things can happen: The couple divorces and each begins to seek another partner (with whom they are probably going to have to face the same issues). The couple works on helping each other to grow and heal. The couple gets stuck in the resentment and lack of fulfillment and lives in a pitched but muted battle.

There is another way in which the bond of romantic and sexual love can help people to grow and develop. Dr. David Schnarch, author of *Passionate Marriage*, has spent his life working with couples. He has found that intimate sexual relationships are a wonderful catalyst for helping people learn how to assert themselves without blaming others or pushing others away. He teaches people how to be involved in intimate relationships while, at the same time, honoring their uniqueness, aloneness and separateness. He makes a distinction between other-validated intimacy and self-validated intimacy. In other-validated intimacy, a person depends on the other person for affirmation and is thus vulnerable to being hurt and upset. Self-validated intimacy involves a person disclosing him or herself in the presence of the other. In order to practice self-validated intimacy, Schnarch teaches his clients how to soothe themselves, because if they depend on others to be appreciated, they have given away a critical resource for taking care of themselves. He teaches people how to ask for what they want without becoming overly affected by their partners' responses. He teaches them how to stand their ground without becoming resentful and reactive. He helps them realize that their partners are doing what they're doing or not doing what they're not doing for their own reasons that may have little to do with them.[5]

The sexual bond is a great resource for this kind of growing and healing, precisely because it is so powerful. The deep knowledge and pull of that power enables people to stay in relationships and work on them even when the going is rough. This is why I believe sexual attraction is a good, if not essential, foundation for marriage.

Soothing oneself: A key to satisfying intimacy

Schnarch found that it is important for people in intimate relationships to learn how to soothe themselves, because if they don't, they depend too much on the other person. How do you learn to soothe yourself?

The first step is to give yourself credit for how far you have come, for the trials and tribulations you have undergone and survived. Even those of us who have had what appears to be an easy time have had to overcome obstacles and deal with adversity. To have come this far is a feat worthy of respect.

The second step is to accept, perhaps even love, the ways in which we are stupid, dense, selfish, blind, mean, weak, immature, flawed and otherwise imperfect. This is a big step and important, because if we don't do this, we get caught up in resisting this truth and we spend lots of energy in covering up, defending and beating ourselves up. Again, psychiatrist author M. Scott Peck defines evil as people who don't own their imperfections. The other drawback of not being able to accept our imperfections is that such resistance keeps us from getting better.

The third step is to know the truth of a dictum which I learned from my practicum supervisor, a wise and experienced psychotherapist. He said, from time to time, "Everyone is doing the best they can in their own situation, as they perceive it, with the resources they have."

Here again we are faced with the need to embrace the fundamental paradox that nobody can be blamed for his or her behavior, because he or she didn't choose his or her parents, but everyone is responsible for his or her behavior, because accepting that is the only way people can improve.

The fourth step is to find and regularly use a method for quieting yourself down and going inside yourself. This can be as simple as taking fifteen minutes to sit in silence and reflect and allow whatever comes into your mind to come in. It can be yoga, zazen, monastic practice, Quaker silent meeting or any of a hundred ways of doing it. Here is a simple meditation that you can use to quiet down and listen to that still, small, wise voice inside of you:

Awareness of Breath

1. Assume a comfortable posture lying on your back or sitting. If you are sitting, keep your spine straight and let your shoulders drop.

2. Close your eyes if it feels comfortable.

3. Bring your attention to your belly, feeling it rise or expand gently on the in-breath and fall or recede on the out-breath.

4. Keep the focus on your breathing, "being with" each in-breath for its full duration and with each out-breath for its full duration, as if you were riding the waves of your own breathing.

5. Every time you notice that your mind has wandered off the breath, notice what it was that took you away and then gently bring your attention back to your belly and the feeling of the breath coming in and out.

6. No matter how many times your mind wanders away from the breath, your "job" is simply to bring it back to the breath every time, no matter what it becomes preoccupied with.

7. Practice this exercise for fifteen minutes at a convenient time every day, whether you feel like it or not, for one week and see how it feels to incorporate a disciplined meditation practice into your life. Be aware of how it feels to spend some time each day just being with your breath without having to do anything.

Another way of quieting down and giving your mind some space in which it can stretch and flex is regular aerobic exercise: running, jogging, biking, swimming, cross-country skiing or skating for at least thirty minutes at a time. There is something about getting your heart beating at 80 percent of maximum for thirty minutes that frees the mind and allows it to open up.

Managing your boundary: Becoming a wise gatekeeper

One key to getting along with other people without giving up too much of yourself, to taking care of yourself without hurting yourself or others, is learning how to manage your boundary. The boundary is that space between you and others. It's where you end and the other starts. We are most effective when we can control or manage that space in a flexible way depending on the situation. When we are unable to manage our boundary effectively, we let other people's reactions and behaviors have too much effect on us. We allow other people to keep us from doing what we want to do. We allow other people to make us feel bad, angry, guilty and sad. Or we put up such an impenetrable barrier that we are unable to receive messages and signals from other people and, thus, are unable to learn how to operate effectively in the world. Some people who are unable to manage their boundaries retreat totally from others and become hermits and vagabonds. One view of paranoid schizophrenia is that it is an extreme reaction by people who can't manage their boundaries.

Here's how Pat Ogden, a psychotherapist who works with trauma victims, describes boundary management: "Through boundaries, we are able to screen input from the world, to know what input is appropriate to let in and assimilate and what input we need to keep out. With healthy boundaries we keep ourselves from accepting subtle or overt kinds of abuse and we also are sensitive to and respectful of the rights and boundaries of others."[6]

We can be both under-bounded—in which case we allow other people to affect us too much and become enmeshed with others—and over-bounded—in which case we protect ourselves so vigorously and carefully that we cut ourselves off from others.

People who are good at managing their boundaries teach other people how to treat them. They are not hurt easily by other people, because they know that the behavior of others is usually more about those others than it is about them. They know that, if they are just living their lives as they want to live them, moving forward on their roads, taking their journeys, then how other people react to them is the business of the other people, not of themselves. They have learned that it works best if they stay on their side of the street and let other people stay on their own side of the street.

Boundary management is especially crucial in intimate relationships. When young people are jilted by their lovers, they often compound the pain of loss by believing that there is something wrong with them, that they are deficient somehow. Older people have learned that lovers who leave usually leave for their own reasons: They want more freedom. They are tired of being in the relationship. They yearn for the excitement of being single. Thus, older people can feel the pain and anguish of loss without compounding it by beating themselves up.

Here's an exercise to help you learn how to manage your boundary better:

Managing Your Boundary Exercise

1. Make two lists. List 1 is a list of people you feel you have to please. List 2 is a list of people who make you upset, angry, afraid or jealous.

2. Pick one person from List 1. Ask yourself what it is you have to do to please that person and how you would know if s/he were pleased. Write down the answers.

3. Role-play a conversation with that person in which you play both yourself and the other person. You can do this either by writing your conversation as a dialogue or by using a version of the Chair Technique. To use the Chair Technique, set up two chairs facing each other. When you are in the first chair you are playing yourself; when you are in the other chair, you are playing the other person. As you carry out the conversation you change chairs. In the written dialogue or spoken conversation, say that you are making a choice to please the other person. Write or say what you are willing to do and what you are not willing to do. Imagine how he or she will respond and either write the responses or say them in the spoken conversation. You don't know how he or she will really respond, but there is value in imagining how he or she would respond and carrying out the pretend conversation with him or her.

4. Pick a person from List 2. Using a written dialogue or the Chair Technique, role-play a conversation with the person in which you tell him or her that you are responsible for your reaction to him or her. Tell the person what you want from him or her and inquire what he or she wants from you.

5. When you have these conversations, don't worry too much about how you sound or how accurately you are depicting the other person. Just do it and see what happens. When you're finished, ask yourself what this might be telling you about how you manage your boundary and what you can do to manage it more effectively.

We've been exploring various techniques for managing your boundary. These techniques are useful, but they are frequently a reflection of a principle which can be even more powerful. The principle behind these techniques is: In order to live healthy lives we have to relate to other people. Loving and working as we want to involves living with others. Because we are unique and different in many ways, we are always going to be in conflict with others. The only way to avoid such conflict is to be hermits or to create fantasy worlds of our own in which we don't have to deal with others, i.e., become psychotic. Thus, conflict is a normal, unavoidable byproduct of active, energetic, bright, ambitious people living together. It is also a very useful signal that something is wrong and needs to be addressed. The best thing to do is notice conflict quickly, acknowledge it and address it in a way that honors the unique interests of the people involved.

Chapter 14

YOU AND YOUR SHADOW

The world is complicated and people are complicated. That can make life interesting, rich, exciting and scary—but not simple. Living well requires letting the complexity in, integrating it and using it without letting it overwhelm us. Let's focus now on two ways of doing that:

1. Finding the middle ground within the polarities with which we live. Examples: the desire to be both independent and dependent; to be part of a team but to stand out; to be tolerant of others but also to fiercely defend our territory.
2. Acknowledging and owning the various parts of ourselves—especially the parts that we don't like and want to keep hidden from others.

Finding the middle ground by honoring both sides

We are complex, multi-faceted animals with intricate, fine-tuned and versatile bodies/minds. One requirement of living well is learning how to use the complexity for our benefit rather than let it overwhelm and confuse us. This requires being able to manage effectively within all of these polarities with which we live. Do we want to be independent or dependent—or somewhere in between? Do we want to lead or follow? Do we want to be active or passive, initiating or reflecting, advocating or inquiring? Shall we be cold and reserved or warm and engaging? Tough or easy? Tolerant or demanding? Open or closed? Aggressive or submissive? Unfortunately, the answer is: It depends.

It depends on the situation we're in, what we want, how we feel, our long-range plans, our short-range predicaments, where we are in our lives, where we are going, where we have been.

Friedrich Perls, the developer of Gestalt therapy whom I mentioned earlier, was interested in how people stop themselves, how they keep themselves from doing what they want to do, how they "dumb" themselves. One thing he found that got in the way was ruminating, living in our heads, overthinking, intellectualizing. He found this was especially true when people were faced with a dilemma—like trying to figure out where to be on the polarity continuum. Perls developed a technique for helping people deal more effectively with these internal dialogues, this incessant arguing that goes on inside our heads.[1]

Exposing Your Internal Dialogue

This technique involves getting the dialogue out of our heads and onto a piece of paper or expressed through our voices. When you are faced with a difficult dilemma such as: "Should I look for a better job or stay with this one that is okay, but which I'm getting tired of?" or "Should I stay married to my spouse or admit that I'm miserable and leave?" Perls suggests that you have a conversation between the two parts of yourself which are at odds. This can be done by writing the conversation down on paper in the form of dialogue in a play. Or it can be done by setting up two chairs facing each other and having a conversation between the two parts of yourself, with you playing both parts. The idea is not to be careful about what you say, not to worry about editing or the words you use but to speak from the heart, in everyday language, directly and simply.

- The more independent and self-sufficient we are, the more able we are to be involved in satisfying, intimate relationships.
- The more we try to avoid problems, the more present they become.
- The harder we try to hit a home run, the less likely we will.
- The more we focus on the outcome rather than the process required to get to the outcome, the less likely we are to get the outcome we want.

How can we learn to embrace paradox? We open up our minds to the complexity of things and to some of the mysteries that we haven't become smart enough to explain. One thing that helps is to substitute *both/and* statements for *either/or* statements, to substitute *and* for *but*. So instead of saying "I want to be married, *but* I also want to be free, independent and adventurous", we say "I want to be married *and* I want to be free, independent and adventurous." Instead of saying, "*Either* I work for myself *or* I'm part of a team" we say "I *both* work for myself *and* am part of a team."

Psychotherapist Thomas Moore wrote about clients who come to him with very difficult dilemmas, such as wanting to be married but wanting freedom, independence and adventure. He advises them to use their imaginations to find a way to honor both sides of the dilemma.[2] That may sound a little bit too easy, like having your cake and eating it too. But my experience is that our imaginations sometimes *can* enable us to honor both sides in a way that gets us enough of both to resolve the dilemma.

When you are facing one of these difficult dilemmas, you can work on it by finding a comfortable place, inviting your imagination and allowing it to discover a path that honors both sides of the dilemma. You may come up with some surprisingly creative and effective options.

Becoming aware of more options can be very helpful. It can open up possibilities of which you hadn't thought. Once you have come up with various options, you may want to use this technique to help with your decision:

Change Foursquare

1. Put the dilemma and the options into words and write them down.
2. Draw a rectangle with four boxes.
3. Label the boxes as follows: Pros of making a change; Cons of making a change; Pros of not making a change; Cons of not making a change.
4. For each of the options, fill in the boxes.

Giving your Shadow a home

The other important step in managing the complexity of our personalities is learning how to integrate the various parts of our personalities—especially the aspects we don't enjoy and would rather keep hidden from ourselves and others. Those parts are what pioneering psychologist Carl Jung called the Shadow. Jung was especially interested in how we deal with these parts of our personality, because he came to believe that the basic drive in human beings was for *wholeness*. His experience as a therapist told him that people have a natural, innate drive to fill in the underdeveloped parts of themselves. As they become older, introverted people begin experimenting with more extroversion. People who lived highly structured and neatly wrapped-up lives take steps toward more openness and spontaneity and those who tended to avoid closure begin to work at tying up loose ends and finishing unfinished business.

Perhaps the most difficult step in becoming whole is coming to terms with the parts of ourselves that we don't like, that we tend to deny, hide and berate ourselves about. As we grow up, parents, teachers, religious leaders, the mass media and other shapers of belief teach us that certain emotions and characteristics are good and others are bad. Some of these evaluations are sanctioned by society and are widely held norms. Others are idiosyncratic to our specific mothers and fathers. All of them tend to be more rigid, dogmatic and certain than is appropriate for healthy development of human beings. As a result of this conditioning, we come to value some parts of ourselves more than others, to regard some characteristics as positive and some as negative. No problem, we say. That is what building character is all about. But many of us become too rigid, too black and white, too compartmentalized in our approach. We end up disowning parts of ourselves, hiding them, covering them up, denying them, making believe they aren't there. We become fragmented; we lose parts of ourselves.

Victoria came to see me with common signs of depression. She was sleeping too much and feeling guilty about it. She was eating too much, suffering from various kinds of pain, having difficulty focusing her attention and feeling worthless. One of the things I have always done as a therapist is help my clients get clear about what they want; not what they need or should have but simply what they want. As we worked together it became clear that Victoria had a powerful desire to pursue a certain career. She had married young, had three children quickly and was a devoted, giving mother. She wasn't doing anything about the career she wanted, because she was still involved in caring for her daughters. She believed it would be selfish for her to pursue her career.

I worked with her to help her realize that the depression was largely a result of her disappointment at not having the career she desired, her fear that she never would and her anger at her children for "making it hard for her." I helped her to see that her desire was quite reasonable, that she had devoted much of her life to being a good mother and that allowing her children to keep her from doing what she wanted to do would keep her miserable and unable to help her children anyway. In some ways, she was allowing her children to make it hard for her. As she became more aware of what was going on inside of her and more comfortable with her "selfishness," she resolved to find a way of pursuing her career *and* continuing to help her children in a less involved way. As she began to act on this awareness, her depression lifted.

There is an even more sinister force at work here. Jung believed that each of us has some evil inside. I like to think of it as the part of ourselves that most clearly expresses our animal natures. It is the part that is territorial, that will kill if threatened, that wants what it wants right now—no matter what. If you want to see it expressed in a particularly raw and ferocious form, just try threatening the children of a human female. In a more veiled but not less dangerous form, you can see it on our freeways in the form of aggressive drivers who ride close to your car's tail even when you have no way to get out of their way.

What's wrong with repressing parts of ourselves that are ugly, dysfunctional or evil?

First, we will tend to project those parts of ourselves onto other people, a dangerous distortion that can poison our relationships. For example, if I disown the part of myself that is set on being better than other people and will do virtually anything to prove it, I will see that characteristic in others, criticize it, be turned off by it, hate them and reject them.

From time to time, I find myself being very critical of other people. *Look at that jerk with the sunglasses. He thinks he's all cool.* Or I'll notice all the mistakes that other drivers make. Or I'll see an old couple walking along the street and think, *Oh, look at that; that poor man didn't do what he wanted to do with his life and now he's all sad and his wife has to put up with him.* When I become aware of what's happening, I stop and ask myself: *What is it about myself that I'm disappointed with? How am I down on myself right now?* Usually, I come up with a useful response. What I had been doing is projecting my disappointment and negativity toward myself onto other people. I had been in the grips of the message that we get from religion and popular psychology that we shouldn't be down on ourselves; we should always be positive and think positively.

Second, by disowning the part of yourself that you don't like, you lose whatever value and power is in it. Since part of why you are disowning this aspect of yourself is a result of forces that are outside of yourself, the act of disowning is itself a distortion. And it may be a costly distortion. Part of my Shadow material is my need to be in the spotlight, to be up in front of people performing. I consider that to be infantile, a symptom of egomania. But there is a positive side to it. By performing in front of people, I may be able to entertain them, even to teach them valuable lessons. I may be able to express myself in ways that are helpful to others. It all depends on how I am when I am in front of other people.

Third, by hiding your Shadow material and not owning it, you lose capacity for empathy and tolerance. You run the risk of becoming rigid, intolerant, coldly moralistic. I imagine that had Adolf Hitler been more in touch with his Shadow material and more open to it, the world would have escaped much suffering. Owning the Shadow helps one become more accepting of oneself and, therefore, more accepting of others. It brings a softness into the mix and helps one become more complete and integrated.

Fourth, when you disown and repress these unwanted and un-acknowledged parts of yourself, you lose the ability to manage them. They take on a life of their own, expressing themselves in ways that are perverse and harmful.

Becoming more accepting of ourselves, especially the parts we don't like, is a great healer. Many of the clients with whom I work become unstuck immediately upon becoming more comfortable with their selfishness, childishness, intolerance, pettiness or anger. Once they acknowledge and accept the truth about themselves, they are able to use those characteristics to find ways of moving forward without hurting the other people in their lives.

This exercise is designed to help you get in touch with some of your Shadow aspects that are hard to accept but can also be helpful to you.

Getting In Touch With Your Shadow

One thing you can do to get in touch with your Shadow is find a quiet, peaceful place, put yourself into a relaxed state and answer these questions:

- When you find yourself not liking another person, being turned off by him or her, what is it about that person that you don't like?
- Where in your life and in your personality do you find those characteristics that you don't like in others? (It helps to be totally honest with yourself in this step.)
- How do you hide those characteristics from yourself and others? When do they break out despite your efforts to keep them down?
- When are some times when you have projected those characteristics onto others, essentially distorted them in your eyes? What were the results of those distortions?
- If you could be more objective about those characteristics, what potential value do you see in them? How could they be used to help you love and work as you want to?

Unearth your evil secret

Another approach to becoming friendlier with your Shadow material is to do the "Honoring Your Evil Secret" exercise. This exercise is based on the work of David Maister, a Harvard professor. Maister spends much of his time counseling students who are about to explore the world of work. He advises these students to get in touch with their evil secrets and to honor those evil secrets in their choices of occupation. Your evil secret is the part of you that you know is there, that you don't like and that you try to keep hidden. Maister gives examples of students who want to be filthy rich or to have power over other people but who are not comfortable with those drives. He encourages them to honor their evil secrets as they make their ways. And he helps them understand that their evil secrets aren't really evil and that they probably aren't secrets either.

Honoring Your Evil Secret

Find a peaceful, quiet place to sit and put yourself into a relaxed state, a listening mode and answer these questions:

- What is my evil secret—the part of myself that I know is there but that I don't like and that I try to hide from other people?
- Why do I think this part of me is evil? Where did that idea come from?
- How can my evil secret hurt me?
- What is the potential value of my evil secret? What power is there in it? How could I harness it to help me?
- If I were to honor my evil secret in my life and work, what would I do? What choices would I make? How can I use it for my benefit and keep it from harming me?

the relative size of the male testicles and the promiscuity of females. Male gorillas have relatively small testicles and female gorillas are not very promiscuous. Male chimpanzees have relatively large testicles and female chimpanzees are very promiscuous. Human beings are somewhere in the middle of the range.

This is all evidence of how basic, essential, instinctual and powerful sex is. We know that people may kill because of it; it is a major cause of divorce and an almost ever-present focus of attention. We are aware of it all the time and it can be the source of much of the pain and discomfort we experience. Because it is so important and powerful it also can be a source of concern and fear. Thus, sex can be part of the dark side. Like other parts of the dark side, it needs to be acknowledged, respected, honored and managed.

I believe this is no excuse for someone to cheat on his or her partner. But it's not going to do any good to see this desire to mate with others as something alien or abnormal or sinful. The fact that a man has a natural drive to mate with more than one woman doesn't mean he has to do it or that he will be hurt by not doing it. But it does mean that he can accept that desire as normal and understandable. Desmond Morris, the anthropologist, states that if we acted on our natural desires whenever we saw a member of the opposite gender, we would approach and sniff around and check him or her out in the ways that other animals do. The only thing that keeps us from doing that is the propriety of cultural norms and the rules of social interaction.

Because it is such an essential and powerful drive, sex can cause pain and discomfort. If we're not satisfying the drive for whatever reason, we can begin to believe that there is something wrong with us, that we are not fully human: *If I can't do something as natural and basic as sex, there must really be something wrong with me.* But many things can get in the way: You may not have a partner. You may not think you're doing it right. You may suffer from impotence, premature ejaculation, orgasmic disorder or vaginismus. It may hurt or be uncomfortable in other ways. You may think you're becoming obsessed with it. You may want to have sex in ways you consider shameful. You may be bothered by being attracted to members of your own gender. You may have lost your desire for it.

On the positive side, sexual satisfaction is a key to feeling loved, valued, admired and affirmed. I believe that giving and receiving pleasure is crucial to feeling alive, vibrant and healthy. You can live without it but not without some feeling of emptiness and dissatisfaction.

If you're not satisfied with your sex life, what can you do about it?

Take it seriously

Consider problems with sex as seriously as you would if you weren't getting enough to eat or didn't have a place to sleep comfortably. Put it at the top of your list. Avoid thinking that you can live without it.

My client Jack came in one morning extremely distraught. He had had a particularly upsetting sexual encounter with his wife Samantha the night before. It had brought things to a crisis point for him. Neither he nor his wife had had intercourse prior to their marriage, which occurred when both were twenty-four years old. They had been married for eight years. His wife had never had an orgasm. He was plagued by premature ejaculation and felt that he was letting his wife down. He was so upset that his need to do something about it outweighed his shame.

I referred Jack to a local sex therapist who had been trained by the famous Masters and Johnson duo. The therapist had a team which included himself, his wife and another female therapist. The first thing they did was teach Samantha how to masturbate and pleasure herself. Then they did the most important part of the therapy: through video, lecture and group discussion with other couples, they demystified sex and, particularly, sexual orgasm. They helped Jack and Samantha to see that sex is a long and gradual continuum that begins with holding hands and touching in the most innocent of ways.

Here's an example of how the conversation might go if you are wrestling with a decision of whether or not to quit a job:

A: I think I'm ready to quit this job. I'm not having any fun at it anymore. I don't want to go to work in the morning. I don't think I'm doing the organization any good.

B: Yeah, but you're good at it. And you've put a lot of time and effort into getting good at it. What makes you think you can find something better?

A: I've always been able to find a job. I'm not worried about that. Maybe not here, but somewhere.

B: But this isn't a good time for you to be changing jobs. Your wife's involved in that business that's just getting off the ground. The children are doing well in the schools they're in now.

A: Well, that's true, but as unhappy as I am, I'm not going to be doing them any good. Maybe I can find something different to do at work—get involved more in managing a project that I can get excited about. I'll have to check that out.

B: Yeah, you could hang in there for at least another year and spend some of that time looking for something better.

Some points to keep in mind while using this technique:

- Don't worry about how you are saying what you are saying, what words you are using or whether you're doing it right.
- Don't try to come up with a solution. Just allow both sides to talk to each other.
- Be direct and straightforward in your speech.
- When you're finished, just let the dialogue sit in you for a while. Don't rush to reach a conclusion or make a decision.

In my experience, there is something magical about this technique. The act of getting the thoughts out of your mind and into the air where you can hear them or onto a piece of paper where you can see them is somehow clarifying. The jumble of thoughts that are mixed up in a confusing ball in your head somehow become more intelligible, easier to understand when they hit the air or the paper—when you can hear them or see them. And hearing your voice helps you know where your energy is, giving you some additional information that will help you decide.

Perls' suggestion is not to try to make a decision based on the dialogue right away but to leave the issue, do something else and let the results of the exercise percolate for a while. My experience has been that the dilemma slowly becomes clearer to me after engaging in the exercise—without my working at it or making it happen.

For Perls, being "centered" means being able to live effectively and appropriately within the polarities, finding the place on the continuum that helps you do what you want to do, meet the need that is uppermost in your body/mind and live the way you want to live.

Embrace the paradoxes

Another part of managing this balancing act is learning how to embrace paradox. Paradoxes are things that are true but somehow defy logic or don't make sense; they are situations in which two things are true which logically can't both be true. Here are some examples:

- Since our behavior is a result of something we didn't have any control over (who our mother and father are), we are not responsible for our behavior; yet we are the only ones who can do anything about changing it and, in order to change, we have to take responsibility.
- The more we try to impress other people, the less impressive we are.
- The better we are at fighting with our spouses, the more solid and enjoyable our marriage will be.

Get help

Many therapists have been trained by Masters and Johnson and their disciples over the past decades. If you live in even a medium-sized city it is likely that a trained sex therapist is available. Sex therapists can be of tremendous help, not only with sexual functioning, but also with developing satisfying intimate relationships. There are many good books, audio and videotapes available. Take your concerns about sex seriously and use the available resources to help you fulfill this most basic of needs.

Chapter 16

AVENUES TO HEALTH: DEPRESSION

I believe it is possible that the symptoms of "mental illness," painful and debilitating as they are, are somehow functional and potentially useful. Human beings have had plenty of time for natural selection to have eliminated states of experience and feelings that are not useful, that don't have any survival value. Is it possible that, just as physical pain is useful in telling us that something is wrong in our bodies, psychological pain is useful in telling us that something is wrong in our lives and has to be faced and dealt with?

This question of how to regard "mental illness" is a tricky one. If we define health as being able to function well in the world, people who suffer from mental disorders are ill. Severely depressed people are unable to work or to fulfill their roles as spouses, parents, friends and contributing members of the community. People who are experiencing the symptoms of psychosis lead very constrained lives, unable to use their abilities in a wide range of satisfying ways. In that sense, they are sick.

But the symptoms that lead people to be diagnosed with "mental illnesses" can also be seen as wake-up calls, moves by a wounded psyche to protect itself, attempts to maintain the illusion of being outstandingly gifted and successful, attempts to control events and feel safer in the world. Depression can be seen as a protective tactic by a body/mind that has been under extreme stress for months and is in danger of suffering a stroke or heart attack. The symptoms of depression force a person to stop focusing on the outer world and spend some time looking inside. If people who experience manic episodes can learn from those experiences, they can begin to become less hard on themselves and more able to deal with the challenges of everyday life. People who suffer from anxiety disorders can learn to be more comfortable with some of their unacceptable urges and with the fact that they have little control over the things that can really hurt them. If they can find a safe place to be and people who will be supportive, those who experience the symptoms of psychosis can go through the experience and become less afraid of other human beings and less desperate about living comfortably and effectively in the world.

There is a sense in which the symptoms of "mental illness" can be seen as an opportunity for growth and healing. They can be used by people to get in touch with their genuine selves, to become more comfortable with what is really true about them, to learn what makes them tick, to learn how to better manage their thoughts, feelings and intentions and to come out the other side healthier and whole.

In this and the next three chapters I will explore how the symptoms of depression, bipolar disorder, anxiety disorders and psychotic disorders can be used as avenues to health.

Let's explore this possibility by first taking a look at depression, the most common and widespread of mental disorders. The doctor, psychiatrist or other mental health professional asks the client to give a self-report regarding daily symptoms and changes in activities over a two-week period in order to diagnose depression:

- Feelings of depression, sadness or emptiness
- Loss of interest in normal activities
- Significant weight loss when not dieting or weight gain
- Increase or decrease in appetite
- Insomnia or hypersomnia (excessive sleep)

- Psychomotor agitation (jittery, jerky, jumpy stomach) or retardation (slowed down, sluggish, groggy)
- Fatigue or loss of energy
- Feelings of worthlessness or excessive or inappropriate guilt
- Diminished ability to think or concentrate or indecisiveness
- Recurrent thoughts of death
- Recurrent suicidal ideation with or without a specific plan
- Suicide attempt[1]

If the client responds "Yes" to five or more of those questions and if those symptoms are causing significant distress or impairment in social, occupational or other important areas of functioning, the client is diagnosed with clinical depression.

How might these symptoms be useful to you? What might be going on if you are experiencing these symptoms? It seems as if you are very upset about something. Something is not going right in your life. Something is threatening your ability to live the way you want to live, to love the way you want to love, to work (express yourself) the way you want to work. Something precious has been lost. You are concerned about your life, where it is going. Is it the job, the relationship, the children, the demands of parenting, your social status? You're not going to live forever. Maybe you need to do something about it.

It seems as if you are under a lot of stress or perhaps shutting down after being under a lot of stress for a long time. Perhaps this is the body's way of protecting itself from prolonged stress. There are worse things that could happen—a heart attack, a stroke, cancer. In fact, research has found a strong link between high levels of stress and depression.

This seems like a wake-up call, a message that something is not right and something needs to be done about it. The body/mind is saying: "Stop doing what you're doing. Stop focusing on the outer world, on other people, on your spouse, your clients. It's time to quiet down, go inside, take a serious look at your life, get in touch with what is going on. Stop avoiding this by drinking, drugging, working, playing, sexing, competing, winning. You need to make some important decisions or perhaps accept what is true about you and your life and become more comfortable with it. You need to do some inner work."

Perhaps this is a reaction to the loss of something that is very precious to you. It wouldn't have to be the loss of a person, a job, financial security or a relationship. It might be the loss of youth, certainty or a sense of comfort. If something precious has been lost, perhaps it would be healthy to spend some time experiencing the pain of that loss.

How could the painful experience of loss be helpful? I believe that all human faculties which have survived through the thirty million years of human evolution have to be useful. An answer that makes sense to me: Loss is useful, because it tells us what is precious to us. It tells us what we want to protect and nurture and tells us in a very powerful way that we better do what we can to protect and nurture those precious things. Valuable information indeed.

What if depression is a state of being that forces people to take a look at their social relationships and gives them impetus to do something about changing them? That is the hypothesis of Paul Watson, a behavioral ecologist at the University of New Mexico, who states:

> It induces us to be attentive to the structure of our social network: Who has power? Who has what opinions? How do these opinions of different social partners interact to constrain or enable us to make changes in life? Depression may have a social planning function which helps us to plan active negotiating strategies in a sober, ruminative state so we can go out and actively negotiate ourselves into a better social position with the people who have power to help or hinder us.[2]

Edward Hagen, an evolutionary biologist, has a similar idea. In the ancestral situation, when humans lived in small hunter-gatherer

Can you remember back to the first time you held hands with someone to whom you were sexually attracted, how exciting that was? That's the idea. The couple learned the value of pleasuring each other in all kinds of ways—massage, fellatio, cunnilingus, masturbation. They were aided in overcoming the tyranny of intercourse and orgasm and learning that satisfying sex didn't have to include either of those. If each of the partners came away from the encounter feeling pleasured and good, they had done it right. They learned that a man doesn't have to have an erection to pleasure a woman and that a man doesn't have to have intercourse to be pleasured.

I have kept track of Jack over the years and the addition of satisfying sex has made a big difference in his marriage. He went through eight years of dissatisfaction, shame and pain before he got desperate enough to take it seriously and do something about it. Unfortunately, some people never get there.

Masturbate

There are great benefits to masturbation. Not only is it pleasurable, it also keeps your sexual system alive and well. It keeps your desire for sex from waning to nothing. One of the surprises of a recent survey on sexual behavior was that men who were having more intercourse were also masturbating more than other men.[2] It turns out that far from being a substitute for intercourse, masturbation is an enhancer.

Find a partner

You know to whom you are sexually attracted. You may not be aware of how primordial and hardwired that process is, but you know it when you see it. You can feel it in your loins. You know it in your stomach and in the beat of your heart. What you do about that desire depends on many other factors—if you already have a partner, if the other person has a partner, if you live close enough to get together. And there are many more options than we typically consider.

One woman I know is sexually attracted to some of her husband's friends. She expresses that attraction through banter, kidding around and casual conversation rather than sexual contact.

I counsel my clients to be somewhat bold in declaring themselves to people to whom they are attracted. Paul, one of my single clients, became attracted to Dana, a single woman, at a ten-day workshop he was attending. On the last day of the workshop, he went for a walk with her and told her, "I'm madly in love with you." "Really?" Dana replied. "Well, what are you going to do about it?" Even though they lived far apart from each other, they eventually found a way to get together.

When I'm counseling a person who is wondering about getting married, I tell him or her to pay a lot of attention to chemistry. I emphasize the importance of sexual attraction, the powerful desire to have sex, all kinds of sex (including holding hands), with the other person. Learning how to live in intimacy with another person is a long, arduous process. If you don't have that powerful physical attraction between you, it makes it a lot easier to quit.

Open things up

Broaden your definition of sex so that it includes holding hands, walking arm in arm, hugging each other while sleeping, taking baths and showers together and giving each other massages. Here's an exercise that can help:

No Expectations Massage

Buy some massage lotion, scented if you like. Find a warm and comfortable place to be with your partner. Give each other a massage with the understanding that there are no expectations. Whatever happens is fine as long as both of you feel pleasured and good about it. Let things take their course.

tribes, depression may have had value in compelling other people in one's life to make changes that were in one's interest—to induce the members of one's tribe to come to one's aid.[3]

In the chapter entitled "Gifts of Depression" in his book *Care of the Soul*, Thomas Moore writes:

Depression grants the gift of experience not as a literal fact but as an attitude toward yourself. You get a sense of having lived through something, of being older and wiser. You know that life is suffering, and that knowledge makes a difference. You can't enjoy the bouncy, carefree innocence of youth any longer, a realization that entails both sadness because of the loss, and pleasure in a new sense of self-acceptance and self-knowledge. This awareness of age has a halo of melancholy around it, but it also enjoys a measure of nobility.

When, as counselors and friends, we are the observers of depression and are challenged to find a way to deal with it in others, we could abandon the monotheistic notion that life always has to be cheerful, and be instructed by melancholy.[4]

Medical researcher Antonio Damasio found that people who couldn't feel bad couldn't make good use of their reasoning powers. In his book *Descartes' Error*, he describes his work with people who couldn't process feelings because of lesions in the amygdalas of their brains. Not being able to feel bad, they were unable to make good decisions about their finances, business practices, relationships, etc.[5] They might buy a stock and see that it was losing value but, not feeling bad about it, they wouldn't take any corrective action.

There is a sense in which depression can be seen as a sign of health. When one experiences loss, when one's life is not going as one wants it to go, when one is behaving in a way that is hurting other people and oneself, when one is facing difficult obstacles that keep one from loving the way one wants and working the way one wants—in all of these cases depression is an appropriate response, a healthy response. In these cases, being sad and upset, not being able to sleep and not being interested in things that are not relevant to solving the problem is healthy.

However, depression is associated with suicide. It is a very debilitating condition. Severe depression keeps people from doing any of the things that make life worth living—loving, working, playing, expressing, enjoying. Let's be careful not to make light of a serious illness.

We need some balance here. Perhaps depression is like many things which are good and useful in moderate amounts but dangerous and deadly in extreme amounts. Included in that list are the stress response, alcohol, strychnine and water, among others.

Mainstream psychiatrists like to make a distinction between normal sadness (the "blues") and clinical depression. But such a distinction is not supported by scientific evidence. When pressed, psychiatrists will admit that there is no alternative way of diagnosing depression that would enable them to make such a distinction. We are left with asking clients to describe how they are feeling and thinking and what has been going on in their lives that might explain the symptoms and we use their reports to estimate the cause and the severity.

If you are experiencing the symptoms of depression and are thinking about killing yourself, take immediate action to keep that from happening. Go to the office of a doctor or mental health professional and tell him or her you are thinking about killing yourself. Such medical providers are required by law to do an assessment and, if they think there is a serious risk of a patient killing him or herself or of hurting someone else, they must do what they can to hospitalize the person, involuntarily if necessary.

My reason for advising this is that suicide is a permanent solution to what is probably a temporary problem. Someone described it as going to a baseball game and leaving in the second inning, because your team is five runs behind. It's not a rational thing to do. But on balance, anyone who is thinking of killing themselves should take immediate action to keep from doing that.

But what about the more typical, less severe cases, when people are experiencing the symptoms described at very painful, debilitating and impairing levels but not at severe levels?

The first thing I suggest is that you stop. Stop being totally absorbed in what you have been doing and take some time to sit down and ask yourself these questions:

- What has been going on in my life and my reaction to my life that might account for these symptoms?
- Have I suffered a significant loss? It doesn't have to be the loss of a person. It could also be the loss of security, certainty, comfort or clarity.
- Have I been under significant stress for a long amount of time, i.e., two or three months? If so, what has been causing that?
- Am I concerned about my life? My job? My love relationships? My family and my role in my family? My future?
- Am I hiding some truths about myself from other people? Am I feeling as if I have to put up a good front even when I'm feeling concerned about myself and my life?
- Am I living an authentic life, the life I want to live? Or am I living a life that is driven by the need to achieve the dreams of my parents or to be successful in the way my parents wanted me to be successful?
- What am I pretending not to know?

Stopping is hard to do. We are all so busy with our jobs, our love relationships, our families and friends, getting enough exercise, taking care of our health and finding some time for relaxation and fun that it's hard to find time to just sit and hang out with ourselves. That kind of stopping and self-devotion of time is not honored or appreciated by our culture. It might even be seen by others as strange, a sign of weakness or pathology.

Quiet down and listen for the small, soft voice that can give you some idea about what is going on inside. There are many ways, including meditation, relaxation exercises, hypnosis, visualization, etc. One way of helping the process is to use the exercise described in chapter 1 to help you quiet down and get in touch with some of your thoughts.

I'm assuming that these symptoms are meaningful, that they are some kind of a revelation. Something has happened to shake your confidence in your ability to live the way you want to live. You have suffered a significant loss that tells you that life is not easy. It is fraught with difficult choices, dilemmas, fears and threats. This state of being you are in may be the culmination of months of trying to bear a bad work situation, conflict and loss of love in your marriage, frustration over trying to parent difficult children or concerns over financial security, hoping that things will get better all by themselves and that, somehow, you won't have to deal with them.

But it's not going to be easy to pay heed to this wake-up call. Our culture doesn't routinely make it easy for people to take a break, take some time off to reflect and take stock. We put a lot of pressure on ourselves to stay at the wheel, nose to the grindstone, bearing up no matter what.

Make it a priority to get some help from your friends and family in assisting you to take somewhat of a break. It doesn't mean that you have to stop working. But it may mean that you stop working overtime and that you ask others to take some of the burden of your non-paid work as a parent, lover, spouse, caretaker and friend, to cut you some slack. As hard as it may be, if you are feeling depressed it is time to ask for that kind of help.

What if you do pay heed to this wake-up call, you find some time to spend with yourself and you quiet down and reflect but no solutions come to you? You are still lost, uncertain, confused. Here are things you can do that may help:

Go see a mental health professional—a psychologist, counselor, social worker, marriage and family therapist, etc. When you do that, there is a very important caveat which I recommend. If possible, do not go on any psychotropic medication, i.e., antidepressants, mood stabilizers, antianxiety or antipsychotic drugs.

The reason is that such drugs will make it harder for you to get in touch with what is going on, with the essential cause of your symptoms. There are some situations in which it is wise to use psychotropic drugs, but unless you are at serious risk of hurting yourself or others or are so agitated and out of control that you can't engage in any kind of conversation or manage any of your thoughts, these drugs will get in your way.

Psychotropic drugs have debilitating and dangerous side effects. These include mania, restlessness, sexual dysfunction, increased risk of suicide and violence and the loss of conscience. In the case of antipsychotics, they can cause shrinkage of the neocortex, cognitive impairment, tardive dyskinesia, increased risk of obesity and diabetes and early death.

These drugs cause the brain and central nervous system to compensate and thus make it very hard to withdraw from them. Antidepressants increase the amount of serotonin and other neurotransmitters that are in the synapses between brain neurons. The brain senses that and shuts down some of the receptors that facilitate the functioning of the neurotransmitters. When you try to withdraw from the drugs, the brain has changed. It has downregulated its receptors and produces painful and dangerous withdrawal effects. Using these drugs as treatment is associated with a much higher relapse rate than using psychotherapy or other ways of healing.

The mind-altering prescription drugs—e.g., antidepressants, mood stabilizers, antipsychotics, stimulants—work the same way in which many illegal drugs (e.g., heroin, cocaine, methamphetamines, ecstasy) work. All psychotropic drugs work on the receptors that either facilitate or impede the transmission of neurons in the brain.

There's another big problem with these drugs. People who take them may think they are doing well. But that is often not the case. Other people see that they are not doing very well. They are behaving in strange ways, not caring about how their behavior affects other people, behaving in ways that are hurtful to them.

This is because the drugs get in the way of people having an accurate appraisal of how they are doing. Their subjective experience is that they are doing well. But the truth is they aren't.

I certainly think that, with informed consent, people have a right to use these drugs. The problem is that people rarely get all the information they need to make that decision. They don't learn about the other options that are available to them. They don't get accurate information on the benefits and risks of the drugs compared with the benefits and risks of non-drug therapy.

If you can find a psychiatrist or primary care physician who does not primarily prescribe drugs but who will help you go inside and get in touch with what is going on within you and with what is behind your symptoms, that's great.

Mental health professionals can be helpful, because you can say anything you want to them and they are bound by law to respect your privacy. There are only two circumstances in which that is not true. If you threaten a particular individual with bodily harm and the mental health professional thinks there is a serious risk that you will follow through, he or she is bound by law to inform the police and the person you have threatened. The other case is one in which he or she is subpoenaed to testify in a legal proceeding and, in many cases, mental health professionals will decide to go to jail rather than testify.

Aside from those two rare instances, they will not tell anyone else what you say. You can disclose your most private thoughts in the therapy room. You can say things that are shameful, weak, scary, homicidal, ridiculous and embarrassing. If you are with a person with whom you are comfortable and you allow yourself to reveal what you're feeling without censoring yourself, you will begin to hear yourself say things that will give you some clue as to what is going on to cause the symptoms you are experiencing. Some therapists will be able to help you quiet down enough so you can hear messages from yourself that have been blocked for years by all the noise inside. Many therapists are skilled in the use of hypnosis, which is a way of helping you reach a very calm, receptive state that will enable you to get in touch with parts of yourself that have been blocked by that internal noise. You can also do this by yourself through using the Awareness of Breath exercise that I describe in chapter 13.

Most therapists know that the first way they can assist you is to help you become more comfortable with your symptoms, to help you see the symptoms as understandable and potentially useful, not some alien things to be immediately extinguished and banished but, rather, a powerful message from inside that has something valuable to teach you about yourself and your life. If the therapist isn't doing that, I suggest you find one who will.

This is also an opportunity to get in touch with some of the beliefs, assumptions and attitudes about yourself and the world that lurk beneath your consciousness but which, nevertheless, drive some of your behavior and how you react to things that happen to you. Some approaches to therapy are particularly effective in doing this. The best one I know of is Hakomi therapy, which was developed and refined by Ron Kurtz. If you would like to become more aware of that part of yourself, I recommend going to www.hakomi.com. On that Web site you can learn about how Hakomi therapy works and find therapists who can help you.

Another thing you can do if you are feeling depressed is find a Re-evaluation Counseling program in your community. Re-evaluation Counseling is an approach to emotional healing that was developed by Harvey Jackins in the 1950s. It gives people who are in emotional distress a way of discharging that distress by linking up with a partner in a "listening dyad." With the benefit of some easily accessible coaching, each partner becomes a trained listener and, in effect, provides his or her partner with a service which is similar to the service that was provided to me by the psychoanalyst who helped me emerge from my depression. The trained listener or counselor gives his or her partner the opportunity to say whatever he or she wants to say in an atmosphere of acceptance, non-judgment and affirmation.[6] As the members of the dyad become more skilled at helping each other say whatever it is they have to say with whatever emotional expression is associated with it and without judging it or offering advice or solutions, the speaker begins to get in touch with parts of him or herself which have been hidden and repressed and hears words and thoughts that are clues to what is going on deep inside, to beliefs, attitudes, assumptions that have been buried and repressed, perhaps for years. This is an avenue toward becoming aware of what is causing these painful, debilitating and impairing symptoms. The counselor/ listener permits, encourages and assists emotional discharge and, as the speaker discharges emotions that have been repressed for years, the natural, healthy expression of self is allowed to emerge. One of the beauties of the Re-evaluation Counseling approach is that it is not very costly and it doesn't require one to enter into a professional relationship with attendant power differentials that can sometimes get in the way of the process. For more information on Re-evaluation Counseling, go to www.rc.org.

These are two ways you can get help in figuring out what is going on. Inside you are many more. The key is being confident that your symptoms did not just appear. They were caused by something that has happened in your life—it might just be that you are older and are entering another stage of life—and how you are reacting to it.

In the process of doing this inner work, you may become aware that you have been under a lot of stress for a long amount of time. One of the messages we get from our culture is that we should be able to handle whatever comes our way and if we can't, we are weak or deficient. Men are especially vulnerable to being hard on themselves in this way. According to this viewpoint, if you're in a bad marriage that is bereft of love and affection, if you're in a job that you hate, a job in which you are unable to use your abilities in a way you would like to, if you don't have friends with whom you can be genuine and open, if you're frustrated and scared about not being the kind of parent you want to be, well, you'll just have to suck it up and make the best of it. That may be what you have to do but, if it is, you are going to be under intense stress for a long amount of time. Eventually, your body and your mind will shut down or fall apart. It's impossible to stop the stress response and it's not a good idea to self-medicate, avoid what is causing the stress, run away from it or hope that things will get better all by themselves. But what you can do is acknowledge what is going on, have some compassion for yourself and follow the steps that I describe in chapter 10 for dealing with stress.

While you are going through this process of self-discovery, this process of learning what has caused your symptoms and allowing yourself to settle into the seriousness and melancholy of life, I suggest that you be very assertive about allowing yourself to spend quiet time with yourself, taking care of yourself.

Once you have a pretty good idea about what has caused your symptoms, what is behind the way you are feeling, begin to re-enter the world. One good step is to begin getting some regular exercise, including aerobic exercise. In one of the most thorough and well-done studies of treatments for depression, these approaches were compared: antidepressant drugs, psychotherapy, a combination of drugs and psychotherapy, a placebo and exercise. The treatment group that did best in terms of alleviated symptoms was the exercise group.[7]

Another suggestion is to use the "Connecting Bodily Sensations and Thoughts" exercise described in chapter 1 to get some idea about what your next steps should be. That exercise is a very good way of connecting your feelings with your thoughts and using that combination to get an idea of the direction in which you want to go.

This time of reentering the world of work, relationships and busyness is a time for honoring and using one's strengths. You couldn't have come as far as you have in the world without plenty of strengths. The fact that you have become depressed is itself a strength. Becoming depressed is a sign that you care about yourself and other people, that you care about your life and how you live it. It's a sign that you are living in the real world, not some fantasy world in which everything is wonderful, you always feel good and life is easy. For the Freudians, entering the depressive phase is a step toward maturity, a sign that you are taking responsibility for your behavior and your life and that you have the ability to feel both guilt and pride about your behavior and your life. You realize that you are a separate human being on your individual path and you are going to take responsibility for where you go and how you get there.

In one form of therapy called narrative therapy, the therapist encourages the client to see the troubling symptoms as something outside of him or herself and to give it a name—something like "The Dark Cloud" or "The Negative Energy." The therapist then has the client remember the times when he or she was able to manage that force, to keep it from overcoming him or her. With the therapist's help, the client becomes aware of the strengths he or she has used to do that and to remind him or herself that those strengths are part of him or her and can be used to get on the path to recovery. Then the client imagines a story in which he or she uses those strengths to build the kind of life that he or she wants to live. This time of reentry into the world is a time for remembering those strengths and recapturing them for use in making your way in the world.

It's important that you believe that what you are doing to recover is going to work and that you have some faith in the effectiveness of your approach.

Chapter 17

BIPOLAR DISORDER

There has been a tremendous increase in the number of diagnoses of bipolar disorder over the past five years. Unfortunately, many doctors, psychiatrists and other mental health providers diagnose bipolar disorder without paying strict attention to the criteria contained in the *Diagnostic and Statistical Manual of Mental Disorders* (DSM).

In order to be diagnosed with bipolar disorder, a person has to have experienced at least one manic episode. Here is part of the DSM criteria for a manic episode:

- Distinct period of abnormally and persistently elevated, expansive or irritable mood, lasting at least one week
- Inflated self-esteem or grandiosity
- Decreased need for sleep
- More talkative than usual or pressure to keep talking
- Flight of ideas or subjective experience that thoughts are racing
- Distractibility
- Increase in goal-directed activity
- Excessive involvement in pleasurable activities that have a high potential for painful consequences
- Marked impairment in occupational functioning or in usual social activities or relationships with others[1]

This is a fairly extreme state of being. This person believes he or she is capable of greatness and is having the experience of doing great things. He or she is on a roll, not sleeping, spending hour after hour pursuing some goal. He or she is totally absorbed in what he or she is doing and oblivious to what other people want him or her to do or to how he or she is affecting other people. The person is so focused on what he or she is doing and so caught up with the greatness of it all that he or she is liable to engage in very dangerous and hurtful behavior—buying things he or she doesn't need, entering into business deals that are ill-conceived, engaging in financial transactions that are bound to result in substantial losses, having sex with people he or she doesn't know well. And he or she isn't listening to people who are urging caution and expressing concern about his or her behavior. He or she is engaging in business and financial practices which make sense to him or her but which other people can see are very dangerous and unlikely to end well.

What might be going on here? What might be some of the causes of this behavior? How might it appear to be useful to this person? This looks like an individual who wants to have the experience of being great, of acting on a large stage, of playing in the major leagues, of achieving great things. Is it possible that this is a kind of charade, an attempt to create the illusion that one is doing great things or at least trying to do so?

This person is having the experience of not having to make the choices that regular people have to make:

- Will I buy a new pair of shoes or use that money to pay for dance classes for my daughter?
- Will I go have a beer with my friends or cut the lawn?
- How am I going to get married, have a family and settle down and still live a life full of adventure, travel, risk and excitement?
- Should I take this job? If I do, I won't be able to experience the other ten jobs that would be fun, profitable, exalted and prestigious.

- Will I stay in this humdrum job that I have or will I try to start my own business? If I start a business, how will I protect my family from the risk of losing our house?
- Am I going to stay in this backwater town where I live or move to the metropolis where I can excel?
- How am I going to do a good job of being a mother to these two children and also have some fun and adventure in my life?

This is a person who feels tremendous pressure to be great, who wants to impress other people, who wants to win the respect and love of others, to win the race, to be exalted and honored. This is someone who wants to do that quickly, without a lot of sacrifice and without paying a very large price in terms of time and energy.

What might be driving this behavior? How might we explain it? I'm not suggesting that people make a conscious choice to have a manic episode. But I am suggesting that there is some meaning behind it. There is some reason for it. But it isn't a choice that is made by the rational part of the person's psyche. This behavior is driven by a part of the psyche which is deeper and more essential than the rational part.

The questions of why people are behaving in this way, what is driving this behavior and what is the need that this behavior is trying to satisfy were the major focuses of psychiatrists and psychologists who were working during the first half of the twentieth century. Here is what they thought about what was, in those days, called "manic-depressive illness":

Mania is a regression that involves a denial of the loss of the loved one or the esteem of the loved person. For some manic clients, the regression may spread to include the denial of all experience of loss. This is, in effect, the definition of grandiosity—regression to the state of not having to make the kinds of choices that are required in maturation and the required giving up of possibility.

Mania can be seen as a defense against having to accept the losses involved in differentiation—having to accept the fact that one cannot be all things to all people but rather has to make choices about what kind of adult s/he is going to be—and maturity.

Mania is an attempt by a person who has just been abruptly rejected by a person with whom s/he was in an intensely dependent relationship to win back the love and respect of that person.[2]

What kind of early experience—experience between birth and eighteen years old—would cause a person to fall into this kind of a state? Perhaps this person was under tremendous pressure from a parent to be very successful and to increase the prestige and status of the family but didn't have the strengths and skills that it takes to be very successful in the world. Perhaps this is a person who was not allowed by his or her parents to excel at what he or she wanted to pursue but was forced in another direction and expected to achieve great success at something he or she wasn't good at. Perhaps this is a person who knows that he or she is capable of greatness but has been stymied by obstacles not of his or her own making.

My experience tells me that this is a real possibility. I asked one of my friends who has been hospitalized twice with bipolar disorder what he thought was going on. "I had a lot to do, Al. I had a lot on my plate," he replied. I then asked him if he had gotten the message from his parents that he had to do great things. "It was never said, but it was understood," he answered. Kay Redfield Jamison, psychologist and author of *An Unquiet Mind*, describes her father as a very powerful man who became increasingly angry and abusive as he got older and who burdened her with expectations that she would never be able to satisfy.[3]

This is close to what early psychologists who worked with manic depressives came to believe. Here is the formulation of one of them:[4]

The pre-manic depressive is caught in a cruel dilemma. He has been strongly reinforced for dependency and conventionality; he sees himself, other people and the world in black/white, good/bad terms. And he feels pressure to be highly successful at tasks that entail self-reliance, sensitivity, drive, competitiveness, integrity, interpersonal sophistication and self-esteem. Here is how this happens.

During the first year of life, he feels loved and nurtured. Mother is very comfortable with the dependence of the infant and enjoys meeting his needs. But when, around age one, the infant begins to become assertive, rebellious and demanding, the mother becomes harshly punitive. Thus, the child learns that he is loved and nurtured when he is dependent and he is punished when he is independent, defiant and autonomous. This causes "splitting." He comes to see himself and the world in black/white, good/bad terms. If such a child is then burdened with pressure to be successful in the world as a way of elevating family prestige or satisfying a mother or father's desire for higher status, he is in a real bind. He has been strongly reinforced for dependency and conventionality. He is unable to deal with the grays, ambiguity and contingency of the real world. He does not have what it takes to be successful at high levels in the world of business. He feels tremendous pressure to be successful and guilt at not being so. This is a tinderbox for the manic episode.

One way of getting an idea of what is going on with this type of person is to look at the characteristics of people who are more at risk for manic episodes than others. Here's a list of those characteristics:[5]

- Sees things as good/bad, moral/immoral, splits and compartmentalizes and is thus vulnerable to extreme swings of mood in response to minor triggers in the environment.

- Lower in self-complexity and so more susceptible to mood swings in response to life events—especially intensely dependent relationships which are interrupted.
- Deficits in tasks involving response inhibition, delayed gratification and sustained attention.
- On a personality scale, lower in persistence and conscientiousness, higher in neuroticism and openness to experience.
- Dysfunctional attitudes toward goal setting.
- Given to mistrustful anxiety.

There are less extreme states of being which don't rise to the level of a manic episode but which are very similar in terms of behavior and the reasons for it. Examples are: workaholism, in which the time and energy spent on work drives out everything else in one's life, and extreme focus on one aspect of life to the point of not meeting one's responsibilities and obligations, becoming very unbalanced and avoiding issues and problems which need to be dealt with.

The first step when a person is experiencing a manic episode is to help the person come out of the manic episode enough to consider the possibility that what s/he is doing doesn't make sense and is harmful to him or herself and others. This may not be easy. This is a case in which a psychotropic drug may be helpful. Lithium has been used to smooth out mood swings for a long time. I once asked a very experienced psychiatrist what was the best psychotropic drug she knew of. Lithium was the answer. I have spoken with people who were in such manic states that they were unable to slow down their thoughts and were helped enough by a mood-stabilizing psychotropic drug to be able to engage in conversation.

Once the person is able to step back, even a little bit, from the manic state, I suggest that s/he reflect on these kinds of questions:

- What is driving me to be so outstanding, special, brilliant, successful? Where is that coming from? What experiences have I had in my life that might explain this?

- What about myself am I refusing to know, am I hiding from myself, refusing to accept?
- What is so difficult about addressing the real, everyday issues of my life—my job or lack thereof, my love relationships, my parenting responsibilities, my ability to express myself—in the way that I want to?
- What is so hard about accepting the fact that I am just a regular person, part of the crowd with talent and abilities, strengths and weaknesses, gifts and deficits, good and bad but nothing very special or exalted?

I suggest that the person get some help from a psychotherapist in asking and answering these kinds of questions. Once he or she has made some progress on this task and gained some insights into some of the deeply embedded attitudes, beliefs and assumptions about him or herself and the world that are driving this behavior, I suggest that this person address several tasks in more or less this temporal order:

1. Experience the rage at having been pressured, misunderstood, discounted and hurt by parental figures.
2. Experience the sadness of what has been lost, mistakes that have been made, people who have been hurt.
3. Experience the shame of not having been as good, wise, brilliant, helpful and successful as you wanted to be.
4. Develop compassion for yourself. After all, you did not choose your parents nor did you choose the situation in which you were placed. You have just been trying to survive, enjoy your life, feel okay about yourself and do the best you can do as a lover, spouse, worker, parent, etc.
5. Begin to forgive the people who have hurt you. After all, they were doing the best they could in their own situations, as they perceived them, with the resources they had.
6. Begin to develop some of the skills you will need to live a more enjoyable life—assertiveness, using your feelings in appropriate ways, using the stress response to address things

that are getting in your way, finding middle ground, addressing difficult dilemmas, learning to get along with others without giving up too much of yourself. Look at chapter 13 for some practical ways of doing this.

7. Become aware of what you really want in your life, not what others think you should want and not what you think you should want but what the unique separate, different person whom you are really wants.

8. Begin to wrestle with the real choices you have to make and begin to take action to follow through on the choices.

9. Become more effective at going after what you want and enrolling the important people in your life to help you do that.

10. Experience the regret of not being able to do everything you want to do and having to accept some necessary losses. For help with this, you might want to read *Necessary Losses* by Judith Viorst.

There is a more positive way to look at a manic episode. Many people who have gone through manic episodes have come to see them as spiritual emergencies which enable them to break through limited senses of themselves and experience a freer, more holy part of themselves that connects with the higher, more positive, hopeful and spiritual parts of life. Sean Blackwell, who has experienced manic episodes, learned from others and worked hard at understanding them, believes the episodes are triggered by the collapse of a false sense of self and a deeply motivated move by the psyche to resolve a tension between "who you really are and who you think you need to be in order to survive."[6]

Others have used manic episodes as an impetus to seek wisdom and find answers to big questions such as "What are we doing here?", "In what way am I connected to other humans, plants and animals and the universe?" and "How can I integrate the dark, spiritual, unconscious, emotional, irrational parts of myself with the rational part that lives in daylight and has to deal with the world and 'reality'?"

Most people who have come to see the manic episode as a spiritual emergency and who have been able to go through it and learn from it regard it as a crucial step in helping them to become more healthy and whole; a useful outcome indeed. One dramatic example of this truth is the Hearing Voices Network, which is comprised of people who hear voices but have found ways to manage and use them in various ways that are not harmful to themselves or others.

Fifty years ago, it was generally understood that "manic depressives" were very creative people, some of whom fed off their manic episodes to achieve what were, in fact, great things. Some researchers wondered about the connection between creativity and manic depression. They theorized that manic depressives had a unique ability to hold two antithetical and mutually contradictory ideas or concepts in their minds at the same time and that this ability fueled their creativity. They could hold onto and use such opposites as wildness and constraint, vivid and drab, order and chaos, strength and weakness, compassion and cruelty. In other words, the experience of not having to make choices and being able to hold mutually exclusive qualities in their minds fueled their creativity.

Whether the manic episode is healthy or not depends on how it is affecting the well-being of the person who is experiencing it and the people close to him or her. What kind of impact is it having on his or her life? How is it affecting other people in his or her life?

If you assume that all states of being must have some potential survival value, you also assume that there must be some learning that can be associated with all states of being. A person can learn from a manic episode and in this chapter we have looked at some of the ways in which the manic episode might be useful.

People who are using mania to deny the need to make the difficult choices of adulthood can learn how to experience the regret that comes with such choices. Every time we choose to do one thing, we also choose not to do many, many other things which might be more fun, exciting, rewarding, even exalting. People can learn how to settle into and accept the realities that come with growing up. They can learn to accept what is really true about themselves and the world.

People who use manic episodes to avoid having to deal with the mundane, quotidian, everyday issues of life can become more aware of what they want in their work, relationships, social and familial lives and more skilled at learning how to get what they want without hurting, discounting or ignoring the needs of others. They can learn to find the middle ground that is the key to happiness for most of us.

The manic episode can teach people that they can live in a way that is more true to themselves, that they can be free to experience the holy, spiritual, connected sense of life, that they don't have to create false selves and live lives that are constrained by what others want them to be and that conform to conventional wisdom.

I'm convinced that manic episodes, like all states of being, exist for a reason. They are not random states resulting from anomalous biochemical or genetic dynamics. They have meaning and are somehow functional even though not consciously desired. They can be used as opportunities for learning valuable lessons about oneself and as pathways to becoming healthier and happier.

Chapter 18

ANXIETY DISORDERS

In its section on anxiety disorders, the DSM doesn't include a
state of being that is consistent with what we mean when we use
the word "anxiety" in everyday conversation. Rather, it includes
disorders which are more extreme than that (panic disorder, ago-
raphobia, post-traumatic stress disorder), disorders which can be
attributed to specific events or situations (specific phobia, social
phobia, acute stress disorder) or disorders which have very un-
usual or extreme symptoms (obsessive-compulsive disorder, gen-
eralized anxiety disorder).

For a definition of the more common type of anxiety which
visits all of us from time to time, let's turn to *Merriam-Webster's
Collegiate Dictionary*, which defines *anxiety* as:

> painful or apprehensive uneasiness of mind usually over
> an impending or anticipated ill…an abnormal and over-
> whelming sense of apprehension and fear often marked
> by physiological signs (as sweating, tension, and increased
> pulse), by doubt concerning the reality and nature of
> the threat, and by self-doubt about one's capacity to cope
> with it.[1]

This sounds a lot like the stress response defined by Hans Selye
as "the non-specific response of the organism to any demand placed
upon it."[2]

Again, I am assuming that any state of being that humans can experience must have some survival value, must contribute somehow to our health and happiness. So what would be the usefulness of anxiety or the stress response? This, I think, is relatively easy to answer.

Anxiety and the stress response tell us that something is threatening us or being demanded of us that is going to be difficult to deal with. Something is getting in the way of our ability to love the way we want to love, work (express ourselves) the way we want to work, enjoy the way we want to enjoy, live the way we want to live. The symptoms tell us that energy is being built up in our organism to deal with it. The stress response gives us increased stamina, sharpness, strength, pain tolerance and quickness.

It's easy to see how such a response is useful to us. It gives us the resources we need to deal with the threat or meet the demand. It arms us for battle. Useful, indeed! And there is evidence of its usefulness. Recall that research has found that people who are moderately anxious score higher on the Scholastic Aptitude Test (SAT) than people who are either extremely anxious or not anxious at all. People who react to stress by taking action and trying to exercise some control over whatever is causing it are healthier than people who avoid it or distract themselves.

More than any other states of being I can think of, anxiety and stress are useful in moderate amounts and intensity and extremely harmful in excessive amounts and intensity, because if you don't use the energy, strength and stamina that anxiety and stress give you, you will get sick and depressed and, in extreme cases, die or kill yourself. Threats and demands such as unhappy marriages which include children and houses, depressing jobs that must be retained for the time being, the challenges of parenting difficult children and troubling conflict with siblings, parents, coworkers or spouses can cause this kind of danger.

If I could do one thing to improve the health and well-being of my fellow human beings, it would be teaching them how to use anxiety and the stress response. What are the keys to doing that?

Be aware that you are experiencing anxiety and stress. Some people have been so traumatized that they have shut themselves off from receiving messages from their bodies. At the first sign of activation, either their emotions explode or they enter a fugue of dissociation. Those people would benefit from the kind of trauma therapy that is provided by the Sensorimotor Psychotherapy Institute in Boulder, Colorado.

Once you are aware that you are experiencing anxiety or stress, the next step is to allow yourself to know what is causing it. What is the threat or demand that has brought this on? This may take some time and effort. You may have to sit with the anxiety and stress for some time. It may help to sit quietly in a safe, comfortable place and allow your mind to reflect on whatever comes up. It may help to take a long walk in nature, to pay attention to your dreams, to ask yourself, *What am I pretending not to know?*

The next step is to decide what, if anything, you want to do about the cause of your anxiety. If you decide to do something about it, you'll need a plan that includes getting help from others, finding a way of doing it without making things worse, overcoming the natural fear of taking action, dealing with the potential obstacles to success, etc.

What if you decide not to do anything about the anxiety at this time? It's important to find some good ways of using the energy, strength and stamina in anxiety and stress: exercising vigorously; building, fixing and cleaning things; participating in other kinds of creative activity; talking to friends or therapists; helping others; emoting (rolling up the windows in your car and screaming for several minutes, walking on an isolated country road, talking and screaming to yourself, pounding a pillow, beating a tree with a stick); journaling. You need some way of using all of that energy, strength and stamina that has built up within you.

Sometimes, the anxiety and stress will make you fatigued. Don't let the fatigue keep you from taking action. You'll feel better if you do.

Even if you decide to address the threat or meet the demand and use your anxiety and stress to do that, it may be a good idea to use some of the coping methods to drain the energy in your body, because the process of addressing the threat or meeting the demand is bound to create some anxiety. If it were easy to address the threat or meet the demand, you would have already done it.

The one thing you want to avoid doing is seeking comfort and avoiding discomfort in the short run, because if you do that, you won't find out what is causing the threat or demand that is beneath the anxiety and stress and you won't decide what, if anything, to do about it. You'll get comfort in the short run but much discomfort in the long run. You can learn more about how to use anxiety and stress by reviewing chapters 5 and 10.

Social anxiety disorder

Social anxiety disorder (SAD) is an anxiety disorder that has been increasingly diagnosed in recent years. The essential symptom of SAD is not wanting to be around people, especially in situations where it is going to be difficult to leave. The symptom is more than discomfort. If this person is in a room with other people and unable to leave easily, he or she will begin to believe that the other people are thinking bad thoughts about him or her, that they want to harm him or her and he or she will begin to experience somatic symptoms such as sweating, shortness of breath and heart palpitations.

What is going on here? What is bringing this on? This person is afraid of people, has experienced people as toxic, has been made to feel inadequate by other people, is extremely afraid of being evaluated by other people. It may also be that this person has a very high need for approval from others.

The psychology of needing approval from others is somewhat perverse. It goes something like this: If I have a high need for approval from other people, that means that other people can hurt me by withholding their approval. Why would I want to be around people who can hurt me? Better to stay away from them, which makes it less likely that I'll get the approval I crave.

What kinds of early experiences would lead people to have a high need for approval from others? Having not received approval from the most important people in their lives: their parents.

Kelly, a woman with whom I worked, was experiencing the symptoms of SAD. It took a great effort for her to stay in my waiting room if there were other people present. Over time I learned that Kelly had been a caretaker all of her life. As a child she had to take care of her younger siblings. In both of her marriages she had been an underappreciated caregiver. She was continually putting the needs of other people above her own and felt guilty whenever she didn't. The recipients of her care took advantage of her passivity and found ways to justify taking more and more and giving less and less. At the time I was seeing Kelly, she was caring for a disabled uncle in her house. It was not okay for her to take a vacation, go on a weekend trip, not even a night out. She had been socialized into the role of caretaker *in extremis*. It can be argued that she allowed people to take advantage of her, that she wasn't assertive enough to take care of her needs. But where did that passivity come from? I don't think she was born with it.

This was a case in which SAD was driven not only by a fear of other people but also by the desire to hurt other people. Kelly had reason to want to hurt others: She was incredibly angry about having allowed herself to be taken advantage of. But she wasn't an aggressive or violent person. I think one of the reasons Kelly was uncomfortable when around other people was that, deep down, she wanted to hurt them and that was very uncomfortable and scary to her.

I was able to assist Kelly through the use of a technique called systematic desensitization, in which I helped Kelly learn how to relax through meditation, imagery or mild hypnosis; then I had Kelly imagine being in situations that bring on the anxiety and use the relaxation technique to calm down. We did this with increasingly scary situations until Kelly could calm down while imagining the scariest situations. Eventually Kelly learned that it was okay for her to have fun and developed some assertiveness skills which she used to keep from being taken advantage of.

For people who are suffering from the symptoms of SAD, I suggest they spend some time understanding what exactly is scary and off-putting about being around other people in situations in which it is not easy to escape. Where does that fear come from? What in their early experiences—what they experienced between birth and eighteen years old—might account for this? They weren't born with that anxiety. They may have been born more sensitive and reactive than other infants, but that kind of social anxiety must be the result of some other experiences which have affected how they think about themselves and others. The benefit of asking these kinds of questions is that it helps one realize that he or she wasn't born this way. There must be some explanation for it. And, since he or she wasn't born this way, he or she can do something about it.

One suggestion I make to people with similar problems is that they ask themselves, *What is the worst thing that could happen when I am in these situations?* and *Would I be able to handle it if that happened?* One of the things we do is develop extreme fantasies of what might happen. Identifying what the worst thing that could happen is and how we would deal with that can be helpful.

Another suggestion I have is that people with SAD use a technique called *in vivo* exposure with response prevention. The idea is to put oneself in one of the less scary situations and, when one begins to get anxious, to stay there until the anxiety subsides. One of the things that can help with this exercise is self-talk: *I know what this is. I know why I am feeling anxious. I'm clear about the worst thing that could happen and how I can handle it. I can get through this if I just stay here and focus on something outside of myself until the anxiety subsides.*

I also suggest that people who are experiencing SAD do some work on learning to manage their boundaries. As we discussed earlier, this is the line between you and other people. Some people maintain very porous boundaries. They are unable to keep the behavior of other people or their concerns about how other people will react to their behavior from affecting how they feel and how they behave. They are too open, too vulnerable to the

Chapter 15

SERIOUS SEX

Sex is all over the airwaves. It is ever more boldly present in TV sitcoms. Advertisers use it to sell everything from cars to beer to medicine. Few movie plots are without it in one way or another. It is the overarching theme of popular music. Yet, for all of that, it is underrated as a factor in living a good life.

A group of researchers wanted to find out whether or not people were more at risk for heart attack while engaged in sexual intercourse. They got detailed sexual histories from 1200 people who had suffered heart attacks. What they found was surprising: It turned out that people are twice as likely to have a heart attack while having intercourse, but the risk of having a heart attack during such a short amount of time is so small that the increased risk is inconsequential. More significant was the fact that more than half of the subjects had not had sex in the year prior to the heart attack. That is much higher than the 20 percent of adults who have not had sex in the previous year. Their conclusion was that sex might be an inoculation against heart disease.[1]

If it turns out that there is a strong relationship between a satisfying sex life and lowered risk of heart disease, it would suggest that sex is a much more important determinant of health than we have given it credit for. This fits with other evidence I've come across.

Mike, a client of mine, was in a very high-stress job and was having trouble with an enlarged prostate gland. He did not have cancer, but nonetheless he periodically went through the unpleasant experience of having his kidney doctor massage his prostate. After several such treatments, his doctor said, "Mike, you know what's the best thing for your prostate?" Mike looked puzzled. "Ejaculation," the doctor continued. "That's the best thing for your prostate. You want me to give your wife a prescription?" he joked. Mike took the advice seriously and his prostate problems eventually went away.

Another example is the clear relationship between breastfeeding and lower incidence of breast cancer in women. The more breastfeeding a woman has done, the less she is at risk of breast cancer. I'm not suggesting that breastfeeding is a sexual act. But certainly breasts are sexual organs and it seems as if this is another example of the "use it or lose it" dynamic that is so powerful in human health.

I include sex as part of the dark side precisely because it is the most basic of drives and much of sexual behavior is hardwired and instinctual. Here are some examples of how fundamental and essential it is:

Recall the research in which women were asked to smell T-shirts that had been worn by men and hadn't been washed and to pick out the ones that were attractive. It turned out that women were attracted to the T-shirts of men with whom a sexual union would produce offspring with strong immune systems. Apparently, the process of sexual attraction, which seems to be a matter of free choice, is driven by forces more primordial and biologically determined than we originally imagined.

Zoologists have found that, in all species, the gender that is more invested in childrearing is also more careful about with whom it mates. In sea horses, the males are more invested in childrearing and are more careful in choosing mates. In human beings, it is the opposite. Human infants are much more in need of support and nurturance from their mothers than their fathers and human males are much less careful in choosing sexual partners.

Among the various species in the primate family to which we belong, there is a direct and proportional relationship between behavior of others. Other people have very rigid and impervious boundaries. They refuse to be affected by what other people think or how other people are behaving. They are very closed and protective.

Healthy boundary management involves being flexible enough so that you can have a relatively open and porous boundary when you want or when the situation calls for that and you can be more rigid and closed when that is more appropriate.

Here is an example of healthy self-talk that people with healthy boundaries can engage in: *If I'm just living my life the way I want to without hurting other people and other people are having a hard time with it, I'll let them deal with it. I'll stay on my side of the street and they can stay on theirs. Most people do what they do for their own reasons. They may want to blame me for what they are doing but I don't have to accept that.*

Use this exercise to develop a better sense of how you want to manage your boundary:

Boundary Management

- Sit in a chair in an open room. Get a piece of string or rope and put it on the floor around your chair at a distance that feels comfortable to you. This is your boundary.
- Write a note to yourself about how you are going to manage your boundary. It might be something like, "I'm going to trust myself not to let toxic people in and I will be the one who decides" or "I have the power and capability to manage my boundary and it is my right to do that."
- Write another note explaining to other people how you are going to manage your boundary. It might be something like, "I'm going to be very careful about who comes through my boundary" or "I don't have to let my concerns about how other people will react to my behavior keep me from doing what I want to do; I trust myself to know what is right and what is not right."

Panic disorder

What about more extreme forms of anxiety? Let's take a look at panic disorder. Panic attacks are very uncomfortable and scary. All of a sudden you notice your heart beating faster and stronger. You notice some sweating, a tightness in your head or some jumpiness in your stomach. You start thinking, *Uh-oh, what's going on? Something is wrong.* Your heart is thumping loudly. There is a numbness in your fingers and toes. You're having trouble swallowing. You feel short of breath, can't get a deep breath in. Now you're really worried. *Is this a heart attack or a stroke?* You begin to feel faint and are afraid that you're going to lose consciousness. Your heart continues beating faster and faster. You can't catch your breath. You're afraid of blacking out. You're in a vicious feedback loop. The stronger your symptoms, the more scared you get and the more scared you get, the stronger your symptoms become.

This extreme experience keeps you from doing whatever you were doing before the symptoms started. If you were driving a car, you pull over. If you're at work, you escape from wherever you are to find a place away from other people. If you're at a party, you rush outside or find a bathroom. It's easy to understand how a person who is suffering from frequent panic attacks does not want to leave the house or do much of anything.

What is the cause of the panic attack? What is underneath it?

The clearest thing about what is going on is that there is a lot of energy in the body. The body is revving up, gearing up for action. What does the body want to do? There must be something important that the body wants to address, to do something about. There must be some problem, threat, dilemma that is demanding action.

That is what I think is going on: I think people who are experiencing panic attacks are facing a dilemma that is so difficult and intractable they don't even want to know what it is. I work with many clients who complain of panic attacks. At some point in our relationship, I ask them if they can think of any problem or dilemma that could explain the attacks. Hardly any of my clients are able to identify one. I press some of them fairly heavily. Still, they don't believe that there is a problem or dilemma behind the attacks. They feel as if the attacks are coming out of the blue, just showing up in a random kind of way. In fact, one of the symptoms of panic disorder in the DSM is that it feels as if the panic attacks appear unexpectedly, that there is no reason for them of which one is aware.

Recall Moira, a client of mine who eventually got in touch with what was causing her panic attacks. Her experience is instructive. Moira came in complaining of the classic symptoms I have described. At first she couldn't think of any situation or concern that could account for the attacks. But then she mentioned that her son was going to be doing a tour of duty in Iraq. She had no control over the situation and the prospects were terrifying to her as a mother. Her mind refused to acknowledge the dilemma consciously, but her body knew better and revved up for action.

I think all panic attacks are about dilemmas and situations that don't have any good solutions, only less worse ones. With many of my clients it seems clear to me what the dilemma is. Often it involves a difficult, unsatisfying marriage that, for various reasons, is not going to be resolved. Hardly any of my clients are able to identify the dilemma and address it. It appears to me that they are dealing with problems that are so difficult they don't even want to know what they are.

In such cases, I help them learn how to get through the attacks. That involves teaching them how to do self-talk and to focus their attention on something outside of themselves. The self-talk includes messages such as: *I know what this is. This is a panic attack. I've been through it before and I'll get through this one. This is not a heart attack or a stroke. I'll just focus my attention on something outside of myself and this will be over in a minute or two.* Most clients are successful in learning how to do this. But the attacks are still very uncomfortable and often disrupting influences in their lives.

One of the perverse things about panic attacks is that the symptoms are very similar to the symptoms of heart attack and stroke. Many people go to emergency rooms with the symptoms of panic disorder but none of the tests indicate problems related to heart attack or stroke. Research has found that the typical sufferer of panic attacks goes to several specialists before he or she accepts the diagnosis of panic disorder.[3]

I suggest that people who are experiencing panic attacks get themselves checked by a medical professional to see if the symptoms do reflect risk of heart attack, stroke or some other indication of physical illness. Once they have accepted that they are experiencing panic attacks, I suggest they learn how to get through the attacks without drastic action—leaving work, driving to the emergency room, etc. As I described, the way to do this is to use self-talk and focus on something outside of yourself until the panic subsides. Most panic attacks last for fewer than three minutes, but they are excruciatingly scary and uncomfortable.

Then people should reflect on these questions:

- **Is there a dilemma I am facing that is so difficult and intractable that I don't even want to know what it is?**
  The most likely suspects are your love relationships, including parenting your children, and your work.
- **Is there a dilemma I am facing that is so difficult that there's no way there is a good answer to it?**
  Although there may not be a good answer to it, there may be a less bad one. Example: As I mentioned, I worked with several women who were experiencing panic attacks. It was clear to me that they were in very difficult and unsatisfying marriages and that they were not going to leave the marriages. They did not accept that dilemma as the cause of their panic attacks. While there may have been no good solution to the problems they were facing—they had children, depended on their husbands financially and had religious and cultural aversions to divorce—there may have been some other acceptable ones. They may have been able to find ways of building more satisfying lives for themselves

without leaving their marriages: spending time with friends, taking classes, becoming involved in art, starting exercise routines, playing sports. Even taking those steps would have been difficult, because it would have required defying their husbands and using some assertiveness skills, but it seemed to be a way of finding a middle-ground solution that might have worked for them.

- **What am I pretending not to know?**

    This question assumes that there are some truths about us and our lives that we hide from ourselves, because if we were aware of them, we would have to take some action that is scary and dangerous. This is a real dilemma. Either we keep these truths hidden from ourselves (not intentionally), we become aware of them and have to take some scary and dangerous action or we accept what is true: that we are not going to take that scary and dangerous action but, instead, are going to live with the situation the best we can.

Becoming aware of the dilemma that is causing the panic attacks is not easy. But I'm convinced that panic attacks are the body getting revved up to deal with a difficult problem and that the best thing you can do is figure out what that dilemma is and either try to do something about it, i.e., find and implement the better solution, or decide not to do anything about it and work at building a satisfying life around it.

Obsessive-compulsive disorder

Perhaps the most troubling and perverse of the anxiety disorders is obsessive-compulsive disorder (OCD). Here is part of the DSM's diagnostic criteria for OCD:

- Obsessions (recurrent and persistent thoughts, impulses or images)
- Attempts to ignore or suppress such obsessions or to neutralize them with some other thought or action

- Compulsions (repetitive behaviors or mental acts that the person feels driven to perform in response to an obsession)
- The behaviors or mental acts are aimed at preventing or reducing distress or averting some dreaded event or situation
- The obsessions or compulsions cause marked distress, are time consuming or significantly interfere with the person's normal functioning, activities or relationships[4]

Again, assuming that all states of being and behavior must somehow be meaningful, must have some survival value, what might be the meaning or usefulness of this kind of experience?

One possible answer is that this kind of excessive hand washing, ordering things, checking and going through rituals may be a way of dealing with the uncomfortable truth that we don't have any control over the things of which we really need to be afraid. We don't, for example, have control over other motorists whose behavior may maim or kill us, over accidents and natural or man-made disasters, over the safety of an airplane flight or over some dangerous illnesses that have genetic origins. The repetitive behavior may give us the illusion of having control over things so that we don't have to experience the discomfort of realizing that we actually don't.

As for the intrusive thoughts, perhaps they are useful in that they enable us to avoid having to take responsibility for making decisions and addressing the difficult, real problems of everyday life—dealing with love relationships, jobs, coworkers, bosses, children, financial difficulties, moral dilemmas, competing priorities. Since we deal with these kinds of problems all the time, perhaps we lose sight of how difficult they can be. They often involve conflict with other people. They often require us to make decisions and choices that involve necessary loss and understandable regret. Carl Jung defined mental illness as "the avoidance of suffering." Some human beings will go to great lengths to avoid dealing with the difficulties of the real world.

Psychiatrist and researcher Jeffrey Schwartz and his colleagues at UCLA Medical Center helped a group of people who were experiencing the symptoms of OCD by teaching them how to change their attitudes toward their thoughts. They taught these people how to create distance between themselves and their thoughts and to realize that they could make a choice about whether or not they paid attention to those thoughts. They learned how to say to themselves, *Oh, there's a thought that was created by my brain. I don't have to pay attention to it if I don't want to.*[5]

Here's what I suggest for people who are experiencing the symptoms of OCD:

- Work at becoming more comfortable with the fact that you have no control over things that can really hurt you. Once you can do that, you may be able to stop being so afraid of the things you do have control over—a way of having the illusion of control over the things you don't have any control over.
- Work at becoming more comfortable and skilled at handling the everyday issues that we all need to deal with—making a living, entering into love relationships, working and finding ways of expressing yourself that are enjoyable, even if that requires upsetting some other people. Work at becoming less of a perfectionist, less demanding and judging of yourself and, rather, accepting of the fact that you're going to make mistakes and come up short and that is a way of learning and getting better.
- Get some help from someone in doing this work. It doesn't have to be a professional, but it does have to be someone whom you trust and who is willing to confront you about behavior that is not working.

Post-traumatic stress disorder

What about post-traumatic stress disorder (PTSD), perhaps the most debilitating of the anxiety disorders? What might be its meaning and usefulness?

Here is a portion of the DSM symptoms of PTSD:

- Recurrent and intrusive distressing recollections of the event, including images, thoughts or perceptions
- Recurrent distressing dreams of the event
- Acting or feeling as if the traumatic event were recurring
- Intense psychological and/or physiological distress at exposure to internal or external cues that symbolize or resemble an aspect of the traumatic event
- Difficulty falling or staying asleep
- Irritability or outbursts of anger
- Difficulty concentrating
- Hypervigilance
- Exaggerated startle response[6]

These symptoms appear to be designed to help the person avoid the psychic and physical pain of the traumatic experience and to avoid a recurrence of the trauma. They also appear to urge the person to relive the experience. It makes sense that people would want to relive traumatic experiences. Typically, people who suffer trauma carry some (usually irrational) guilt about it, believing that they somehow contributed to it happening or that they could have done something about it. Reliving the experience holds out the possibility of resolving the guilt or imagining a different outcome, somehow making more sense out of the incident and coming to a more realistic appraisal of it.

James Pennebaker, chair of the Psychology Department at the University of Texas, has done recurring research on this subject in which he gives a group of students a writing assignment. Half of the students are assigned to write about the most traumatic experiences of their lives. Half are assigned to write about what they are going to do during summer vacation, where they are going to graduate school or some similar innocuous topic. They write for thirty minutes a day, three days in a row. For the next six weeks, their immune systems are evaluated through blood assays and the number of trips to the health clinic is determined. Every time he has done this study, Pennebaker has gotten the same results: The students who write about the most traumatic experiences of their lives have stronger immune functioning and make fewer trips to the health clinic. The reason for this outcome is not clear. One explanation is that as the students write about their traumas, they begin to make more sense of them, develop a more realistic appraisal of them and better integrate them into their lives. This explanation is based on a review of their writing, which indicates a daily progression in this direction.[7]

The value of reliving the traumatic experience in a safe, non-threatening way is also congruent with some of the recently developed approaches to helping trauma victims. In one approach, victims learn how to notice and follow their bodily sensations. Then they are guided to use their imaginations to recall the moment just before the traumatic experiences and to shift their attentions from their imaginations to their bodily sensations. As they notice and follow their bodily sensations, the energy that was trapped inside of them begins to dislodge, process through and eventually discharge. They are encouraged to go back into their minds and see if they can develop more realistic appraisals of the events. Eye movement desensitization and reprocessing (EMDR) therapy helps people go into an altered state and relive the trauma in a way that sometimes enables them to integrate the trauma in healthier ways.

If you are experiencing PTSD, find a psychotherapist who has been trained in helping people heal from trauma. The best group of people I know of is the staff at the Sensorimotor Psychotherapy Institute in Boulder, Colorado. That organization has trained therapists from all over the world. If you call them, they can tell you if there are any trauma-trained therapists in your area. I also recommend seeking therapists who are trained in eye movement desensitization and reprocessing (EMDR) and ones who practice Emotional Freedom Therapy and Thought Field Therapy. These are methods of freeing up frozen energy which results from trauma and using the mind, emotions and body together to heal.

Chapter 19

PSYCHOTIC DISORDERS

In the last few chapters we have been looking at some "mental illnesses." I put quotation marks around "mental illness" because, as we have seen, the symptoms may be unpleasant, uncomfortable, debilitating and dangerous, but they can also be a sign of health, a sign that people are doing their best to avoid pain, protect themselves, feel better about themselves, etc. and the symptoms can be used to become healthier.

However, what about psychosis, with its delusions, hallucinations, disorganization and bizarre behavior? Can those symptoms be a sign of health and an avenue toward becoming healthier? I think so.

The key symptoms of psychosis are delusions and hallucinations. Delusions are beliefs that are not in keeping with consensual reality. Here are some examples I have heard from my clients:

- "I was christened by the first pope."
- "Abraham Lincoln lived from 1868 to 1912."
- "I can jump out of airplanes without a parachute and survive."
- "That man on the corner is reading my thoughts through a device he has implanted in my stomach."
- "My father was the commander of an East Indian army post and I grew up on the post."

Hallucinations are hearing voices, feeling things and seeing things that other people don't hear, feel or see. They often are very intrusive and troubling, telling people they should kill themselves or others, they are no good or they deserve to die. They can also be intrusive but not troubling, telling people, for instance, that they have been anointed by God to lead the forces of good against the forces of evil.

Another symptom of psychosis is extreme aversion to other people. In general, people who have been diagnosed with a psychotic disorder do not want to be around other people and will find ways of pushing people away so they don't have to be around them.

I believe that psychosis can be a protective and life-affirming move of the psyche in response to extreme desperation, fear or terror about the prospect of having to live in the real world with real human beings. Psychologist John Weir Perry has worked with many people who were diagnosed with schizophrenia. He came to see that state of being as a deeply motivated move by the psyche to reconstitute itself. These people had suffered a harsh blow to their self-concept and were experiencing an acute sense of negative self-image. In an effort to compensate for a severely debased self-image, the psyche took on the persona of an exalted, powerful figure. Although it can be seen as healthy in the sense that it is more life-affirming than killing oneself or hurting someone else, the discrepancy between the negative self-image in the real world and the exalted figure in the imaginary world sets up an unstable psychic situation full of a sense of unreality and anxiety. Perry states: "It seems that when the psyche cannot progress further into the next steps of experience so encumbered by this very negative self-image—especially at times of great crises of ebullient falling in love or hurtful falling into rejection—a change is initiated."[1]

The person's psychic energy is attracted to the exalted, powerful, capable imaginary persona and leaves the higher level, rational part of the psyche stripped of its usual energy and hence in a state of disorganization.

I believe that psychosis is the psyche's way of protecting itself from having to live in a world full of toxic human beings, a way of avoiding the impossibility of living up to the expectations that have been thrust upon oneself and of taking on the responsibilities of an adulthood that is too scary to enter. I'm reminded of psychologist Alice Miller's dictum that all you have to do to create mentally ill people is: don't let them be who they are and when they get angry about that, don't let them be angry.[2]

Unable and unwilling to live in the real world of real people, the psyche creates its own world and enters into a process of seeking safety, health and wholeness in that imaginary world. I don't believe people choose this experience. Rather, it is driven by a part of them that is much deeper and smarter than their rational sides. If they could use only their rational sides, they might kill themselves or others.

I believe virtually all people who are diagnosed with schizophrenia have been abused, neglected, discounted or dismissed—in some way traumatized in their early lives. It's significant that the first psychotic break typically occurs just as the person is having to take on the burdens and expectations of adulthood. They are not prepared to do that, are terrified by the prospect and find creative ways of avoiding it.

Alicia was a woman in her mid-forties who had experienced abuse and trauma. When she was in trouble or applying for some kind of assistance, she was grounded and lucid. She made perfect sense. But when she was in the safety and comfort of my office she said delusional things. I asked myself, *Why would that be?* I think she was constantly testing me to see how I would react when she said things like, "I was christened by the first pope." I responded, "But the first pope lived fifteen hundred years ago." Then she replied with, "Oh, I mean the pope today." By doing that, I passed her test, because I was willing to stay engaged with her, to play her game, to stay connected with her. One of the functions of the delusions is to push other people away.

One day, Alicia and I were sitting in my office. She looked at me and said, "Al, you look tired." I replied that her assessment was correct and that I was tired. "You need to talk to the moon more," was her suggestion. This helped me to see that one of the functions of hallucinations and bizarre behavior is to make life interesting. Persons diagnosed with schizophrenia are extremely isolated. They are good at pushing people away and finding ways of distancing themselves. They need other ways of engaging with life that are less dangerous than connecting with real people.

Robert, another client of mine, was an eighteen-year-old. He had been abused, neglected and traumatized repeatedly in early life. One day while we were driving in my car, he asked, "See that guy standing on the corner?"

"Yes," I replied.

"He's reading my thoughts."

"Why does he want to read *your* thoughts?" I asked.

"Because I'm important. He wants to know what I'm thinking," Robert stated matter-of-factly. This helped me realize that one of the functions of these delusions is to help people feel exalted and elevated. Hearing voices enables people to avoid taking responsibility for their behavior or thoughts. The schizoid individual reasons, "It isn't me who is thinking that or urging that behavior. It's the voices."

I don't subscribe to the belief that schizophrenia is caused by chemical imbalances or genetic dynamics. That turns human beings into random organisms who have no control over their behavior. Humans are not random organisms. They are meaning-making organisms who are born with powerful desires to love the way they want to love, be connected to others of their species and work the way they want to work. When those powerful desires are frustrated and when it appears absolutely impossible for them to satisfy those desires, they become desperate and, in desperation, they retreat into altered states of being.

I feel that our society mistreats people who experience the symptoms of schizophrenia. Physicians immediately pump them full of powerful antipsychotic drugs. I believe the drugs often get in the way of the healing process in which the psyche is engaged and turn people into zombies and permanent mental patients.

What we should do is provide people who suffer from schizo-phrenia with a safe place in which they can live without any pressure to "get better," "stop saying those things" or "straighten up." A place in which the staff will just be with them as they go through the healing process, help them work through the experience, make some sense out of it, ultimately learn from it and emerge healthier, more balanced and more whole than when it started.

Several years ago I was talking with a clinical social worker who had worked for a facility in which people diagnosed with psychotic disorders could spend the day connecting with each other, creating artwork, doing volunteer work and getting help with housing, employment and income support. "If I gave you a million dollars a year for five years to be used in helping your clients, what would you do with it?" I asked. "The first thing I would do is create a terrific sports and fitness program through which I could help people express themselves through sports, exercise, weight-lifting, etc.," he replied. "The other thing I would do is create a facility in which people who are in their first psychotic breaks could be helped to go through whatever they are experiencing in a safe, affirming place. What we do now is put pressure on people to get back to where they were, get back on track, back in school or to work, back into the roles they were in before the break. That doesn't work. We medicate them and turn them into chronic mental patients. We need a place where the message is: 'Come on in. We're going to help you go through whatever you are experiencing, help you learn from it and come out the other end more healthy and able to engage with the world.'"[3]

Soteria House, which operated in the San Francisco Bay area starting in 1971, was a home-like residence in which people experiencing their first psychotic episodes could live for as long as three or four months in an environment that was both physically and psychologically safe. The message they received upon entering was: "You can stay here as long as you have to in order to feel less afraid and upset and more stable. We're going to provide you with a safe place in which you can go through whatever you are experiencing. If possible we'll help you try to make some sense out of it."

People generally became more stable after about six weeks. As they became more stable they were encouraged to reconnect with the community, attending day programs and classes, looking for work, volunteering, attending therapy sessions, etc. Although Soteria had a contract with a psychiatrist, drugs were not the primary modality of treatment. The primary modality was relationships, helping the residents become more comfortable with other human beings and able to interact with them in enjoyable and comfortable ways.

One study found that the people who were treated in the Soteria House rather than a hospital did significantly better in terms of symptoms, social functioning, employment and relapse.[4] But even though it was more effective, less harmful and less expensive than hospitals, Soteria ceased operations in 1983. It wasn't keeping with the paradigm that was ascendant in modern psychiatry: diagnose on the basis of symptoms without paying attention to what personal and life issues might be causing the symptoms and treat with drugs and, in severe cases, electroshock.

Today there is a Soteria House in Anchorage, Alaska. It provides people in early psychotic episodes with a safe place in which they can be assisted as they go through whatever they are experiencing and be affirmed in the process. One resident screamed in the middle of the night and brought out the police; another has directed violent outbursts at both staff and fellow residents. The staff has learned how to help both these patients feel safe and comfortable enough to live in the house without incident.

There are two other non-drug approaches to helping people recover from early psychotic breaks. Both are based in Scandinavia. The Open Dialogue approach operates in Finland. In this program, as soon as a person begins to exhibit the symptoms of psychotic disorder, a team of professionals brings together as many people from the person's life as they can—parents, grandparents, uncles, aunts, boyfriends and girlfriends, lovers, bosses, teachers, friends, coaches. This group meets on a daily or every-other-day basis for two to three weeks. The professionals facilitate the meetings. Their goal is to help the group develop a shared understanding of what has happened, how it has happened, what triggered it, what some of the forces behind it are. People are encouraged to tell stories, their own as well as stories of others, and to talk about their relationships with the patient and the patient's family. From time to time the professionals will stop the meeting and talk among themselves in the presence of everyone else. They wonder about what has happened, discuss some ideas about where the problem lies and how things have reached this point. Slowly, a shared understanding develops of what has happened, how it has happened, why it has happened and what might be some helpful ways of proceeding. All treatment decisions are made in the presence of the group, with group input.

The Open Dialogue approach reports a successful recovery rate of about 80 percent compared with recovery rates of less than 20 percent in the United States.

The Healing Homes program operates in Gotheburg, Sweden. It places people who are experiencing psychotic symptoms with farm families who have volunteered and been trained to provide safe and affirming places in which patients can go through the experience. The families receive intensive supervision from professional therapists and the clients receive psychotherapy. Again, the modality of treatment here is relationship and slow reentry into the world. Clients are helped to become comfortable in the farm families and to begin contributing slowly to the work of the farm.

I suggest that people who are experiencing psychotic symptoms find a safe, affirming place in which someone can help them through what they are experiencing. I also suggest that they find one person—a recovered peer, a friend, a counselor who is willing to work outside of the box—who will be available to them on a 24/7 basis and who will stay connected with them no matter what and no matter where—jail, hospital, group home, etc. Having this kind of relationship with one person is important, because as people suffering schizophrenic episodes begin to recover, they can backslide. They could be at work and something happens that will set them off. If this occurs, they will need to connect with someone who can help them get through the episode without undue harm. If they go through such a crisis, overreact and end up in a hospital, they will need someone on whom to rely, who will advocate for them so they don't fall back into the medicated, chronic mental patient trap.

Finally, I have a suggestion for the families of people who experience psychotic symptoms. Read a book entitled *A Way Out of Madness: Dealing With Your Family After You've Been Diagnosed with a Psychiatric Disorder* by Matthew Morissey and Daniel Mackler. Use it to be supportive and affirming as your family member goes through the experience.

Chapter 20

ATTAINING PSYCHOLOGICAL HEALTH

I will discuss the three steps to psychological health:

1. Become aware of what's true about yourself and work at becoming comfortable with it.
2. Go after what you want.
3. Stay connected.

Become aware of what's true about yourself and work at becoming comfortable with it

Ask yourself these questions:

- What do I want?

    This is a very important question and one which we've been socialized to avoid. Somehow, we've learned that there's something selfish and somewhat cheesy about focusing on what we want. As we've seen, most of us want to love the way we want to love and express ourselves—use our abilities— the way we want to express ourselves. If we get to do that, other people are going to benefit. Knowing what we want is a crucial first step. Corollary questions are: What is keeping me from feeling pretty okay about my life? What is missing from my life?

- How do I stop myself from getting what I want?
  We all find ways of stopping ourselves from getting what we want. We can use negative thoughts, irrational fears, manic episodes, obsessions, etc., to sabotage ourselves.
- What am I afraid of?
  One of the ways of staying afraid is not knowing what we're afraid of. It's worthwhile to take some time getting clear about what exactly you are afraid of. Once you're clear about that you can decide whether or not you want to walk with that fear and you can ask yourself: *What is the worst thing that could happen if I walk with this fear?*
- In what ways do I feel inadequate?
  All of us have some weaknesses to overcome, some perversity to manage. In his book *The Path of Least Resistance,* Robert Fritz tells us that if we get clear about where we want to get and where we really are, we will automatically begin moving toward where we want to get and doing what we have to do to get there. In his book *Mastery,* George Leonard describes in detail the process of getting very good at whatever you want to be good at.
- What am I pretending not to know?
  We are all pretty good at this kind of willful ignorance. It makes sense. Why would I want to know something that means I will have to do some hard work, take some risks, admit some things I don't want to admit, upset other people, etc.? But keeping ourselves in the dark is not going to help us get where we want to get. This is a courageous step and a crucial one.
- What am I hiding from other people?
  As we've discussed, we all have our "evil secrets" which we try to hide from others. Unfortunately, we're seldom able to do that and what we think is "evil" isn't evil at all. It's just that we've been told by our culture, parents, teachers or clergy that it is evil. But we can spend a lot of energy trying to hide it, sometimes to the point of exhaustion.

- When I do things to hurt myself, when things happen that I didn't want to have happen, what are some of the hidden, deep down beliefs, attitudes and assumptions about myself and the world that are driving that behavior?

  As we've seen, this is a tough one. How can we be aware of these forces when they are hidden deep beneath our consciousness? Here is the most practical way of doing this; whenever something happens to you that you didn't want to have happen, something hurtful and difficult, ask yourself these questions:

  - How did I contribute to this happening?

  - Why might I have wanted this to happen? Is there any possible way in which I might benefit from this, in which it might enable me to avoid something I am afraid of or get me something that I want?

  - Since I contributed to this happening and yet didn't want it to happen, what can that tell me about some of the forces—beliefs, attitudes, assumptions—that are driving my behavior?

  - What are my strengths? How have I used them in the past and how can I use them now to get what I want?

Take an inventory of the times in your life when you have overcome difficulties and obstacles, when you have successfully confronted challenges. How have you done that? What are the skills, knowledge and abilities that you have used to do that? How can you put them to work now?

There are two processes that can be very helpful to you in doing this work of becoming aware of what is true about yourself and more comfortable with it. First is receiving the valuable messages from your feelings. We have seen how anger, sadness, jealousy, anxiety and fear can help us know what is threatening us, what we want to avoid and get rid of, what is precious to us, what we want and what we need to do that is going to be hard.

Second is remembering that the stress response is helpful. It tells you in a visceral way that there is something that is threatening your ability to love the way you want to love and express yourself the way you want to express yourself. It tells you that you are facing the need to do something that is going to be hard to do. And it gives you the energy, insight and sharpness needed to do it.

Go after what you want

Once you are clear about what you want, it's time to go after it. This doesn't necessarily mean that you will do anything rash or precipitous—leaving your marriage or your job, moving to another city—it just means that you will start taking steps toward living more the way you want to live. They can be slow, even steps or they can be more quick and dramatic.

In his book *Care of the Soul*, Thomas Moore writes about middle grounds. He describes people who come to him troubled by the impossibility of "having it all." Moore tells of a man who wants the comfort and stability of being in a conventional marriage but also wants adventure, excitement and risk in his life. He works with the man on finding a middle ground, some way of having both of those in his life. It may mean taking a road trip every once in a while or getting involved in intensely competitive sports or taking an occasional trek into the wilderness with some friends.[1]

In my therapy practice, I have worked with a number of women who were troubled by the narrowness and dryness of their lives. Their children had started school and they wanted to broaden and enrich their lives, but their husbands didn't want them to change or grow. I worked with them on ways they could begin to step out—going to lunch with friends, taking a course at the community college, getting a part-time job, joining a sports team or a gym. For some of them this required developing some assertiveness skills they needed in order to do what they wanted to do even though their husbands didn't want them to.

There are more options than we are aware of; for example, some married couples manage to make their relationships work while living on different continents. Kyle, a college student, made it a priority to spend time every evening having fun with his friends. He crafted this schedule: Go to class from 9 A.M. to 2 P.M., sleep from 3 P.M. to 6 P.M., have fun with friends from 7 P.M. to 11 P.M., study from 11 P.M. to 2 A.M., sleep from 2 A.M. to 8 A.M. Somehow, he made it work, graduated and was the treasurer of a Fortune 100 company by his late forties.

Pete, although he grew up in a large city, wanted to be a farmer. He and his wife bought a section of land in southwestern Colorado and lived on it without electricity or running water and learned how to raise draft horses, other animals and various crops. They made some money, he as a professor at a nearby college and she as a public health nurse, but lived their own satisfying lifestyle.

One thing to keep in mind is actor Matthew Fox's idea that we need to find ways of expressing ourselves the way we want to. Some of us are lucky enough to be able to get paid to do that. If we aren't, we need to find ways of doing it outside of our working hours.

Going after what you want is very likely going to involve confrontations with people with whom you want to maintain good relationships—wives, husbands, children, parents. This is the time to use the kinds of assertiveness and communication skills that we covered in chapter 13.

Stay connected

One of the hard things about going after what you want is that some people aren't going to like it. Some of the people who aren't going to like it are people with whom you want to remain in relationship. This is tricky. There are various reasons why people may not like your lifestyle choices. Your commitment and movement may put pressure on them to make some changes they don't want to make or to live with situations they don't want to live with. Some people will be jealous. One therapist used to remind me regularly that some people don't like winners. They are much more partial to losers. As soon as you start winning, people will start accusing you of brownnosing, cheating, being "holier than thou," forgetting where you came from, etc.

Maintaining your relationships with important people in your life will require using the assertiveness and communication skills covered in chapter 13 and learning how to manage your boundary. Managing your boundary means finding a balance between being aware of how you are impacting other people and how other people are impacting you but not allowing the reactions of other people or your concerns about how other people will react to your behavior keep you from going after what you want.

Chapter 21

PSYCHOTHERAPY AND
YOUR DARK SIDE

If you feel unable to solve your problems and your dark side is causing your life to be unsatisfying and unfulfilling, seek help.

Psychotherapy can give the client a new, more comfortable and hopeful way of looking at the symptoms that have brought him or her to seek help. A good therapist will help the client see that what is happening in his or her life, no matter how painful, bizarre or upsetting it may be, makes sense in terms of the situation the person has been facing and is facing and in terms of the experiences he or she has had in his or her life. Instead of seeing the symptoms as being alien and something to get rid of, the client comes to see them as understandable, meaningful and, therefore, potentially useful. One of the things I have told my clients is, "If you weren't feeling bad, I'd be worried about you." One of the benefits of this is that the client becomes more comfortable with whatever is going on. Instead of seeing the symptom(s) as weird, defective and bizarre, he or she sees it as a natural response to what has been going on in his or her life and how he or she has been dealing with it.

Clients can become more accepting of whatever is true about themselves. They can let their hair down, stop defending against the truth, stop trying to hide things from themselves and others, stop trying to make believe certain things are true or aren't true.

They can surrender to what is true and stop resisting it. Friedrich Perls came to believe that the first step in making any kind of change was to accept totally and even love whatever was true, no matter how ugly, painful or shameful.[1] One of the helpful things about therapy is that you can say anything in the therapy room with the absolute assurance that it won't leave the room. You can really shelve your inhibitions and express everything that you are feeling. That can be profoundly comforting.

There are various ways in which therapists can help a client do this. One way is to help the client quiet down. Some people are so wired, so hyper-vigilant (for good reasons) that they never quiet down enough to get in touch with the still, small voice within. Oftentimes that still, small voice has some valuable messages for the person. Therapists have ways of helping clients calm down and quiet down, lowering the internal noise level so that the client can receive those messages from within.

Another way in which therapists assist with this process is to encourage the expression of emotion. My client Vicki came to see me because she had lost her ability to feel anything. She could feel neither joy nor sorrow, neither happiness nor sadness. As I helped her become comfortable in the therapy room and to quiet down and get in touch with what was going on inside, she became aware of how difficult her childhood had been. She was an object of competition and jealousy between her mother and father. She was made to feel blame for the problems her mother and father experienced. There was pressure on her to care for her ailing mother. And she had been molested by an uncle. As Vicki got in touch with these truths, she began to cry and spent a lot of time experiencing the sadness and eventually the anger that was inside of her. She came to see that she wasn't to blame, that she was essentially a victim of a situation she didn't create but had to respond to the best she could. As she did this, she became more in touch with her feelings and regained her ability to feel different emotions. Slowly Vicki began to work on her life situation, her work, her marriage and her role as the parent of three children. This occurred over a period of two years.

Many clients who come into therapy have been traumatized. There are two kinds of trauma: life-threatening trauma—being mugged, raped, hurt in accidents, undergoing life-threatening surgery; and developmental trauma—not receiving the nurturance, support, affirmation and care that people need in the first fifteen years of their lives in order to grow into healthy adults. When people have been traumatized as children, they may automatically hide that traumatized part of themselves deep down in their psyches. They present an apparently normal self to the world. But that traumatized part is in them. When they are threatened or struck with a stress response, it comes out and throws them into overreaction and dissociation. I have seen therapists use hypnosis to help such people explore their memories from the early years when they were hurt and have helpful conversations with their younger selves. The therapist says something to them like, "Now that you are an adult, you can give that younger self a place in which s/he can feel safe. You can bring that younger self in out of the cold, give him or her a home where s/he doesn't have to feel so alienated and afraid."

The Sensorimotor Psychotherapy Institute in Boulder, Colorado, teaches therapists how to help clients resolve trauma by reliving the trauma in their bodies. People who have suffered life-threatening trauma oftentimes lose their abilities to get information from their bodily sensations. When the lives of humans are threatened and they can neither fight back nor escape, they, like other mammals, will freeze. When that happens, lots of energy is trapped in their bodies. If they survive, that energy oftentimes stays trapped within. Other animals who survive will spend hours and days shaking and discharging that energy. But social proscriptions keep humans from doing that. Trauma-trained therapists know how to help clients reconnect with their bodies. They spend hours helping clients regain their abilities to experience and notice their bodily sensations. Once a client is able to do that, the therapist will help the client travel back in his or her memories to the point just before the trauma occurred. The therapist then helps the client allow the trauma to be revisited in the body. Reliving the trauma in the body keeps the person from being re-traumatized and enables the energy that has been trapped inside to be discharged. In this way, clients regain their abilities to get information from their bodies and become less likely to overreact and dissociate when they become stressed.

You can see how the clients are learning about themselves, what makes them tick, why they do what they do and don't do what they don't, what they are afraid of, how they stop themselves from getting what they want. An important part of this process is helping clients become aware of the beliefs, attitudes and assumptions they have about themselves and the world which lie below the surface of their consciousness but which nevertheless drive their behavior. One of the hardest things about being alive is knowing that much of our behavior is driven by these unknown forces. How are we going to manage them if we are not aware of them? An important step in becoming healthy is becoming more aware of them. How can therapists help clients do that?

Ron Kurtz and his Hakomi therapists have developed some practical and effective ways of doing so. When Kurtz meets with a client, he is listening, but even more important, he is watching the nonverbal behavior of the client. He may notice that the client shrugs his or her shoulders a lot or touches him or herself a lot, holds onto him or herself. He may notice that the client doesn't make eye contact or tilts his or her head a certain way. He is noticing the habitual behavior of the client and infers that it must be driven by some underlying forces that have a powerful influence over the client's behavior.

Kurtz then helps the client learn how to notice these bodily sensations, become very attuned to what is going on in his or her body, follow it and stay with it. Once the client is able to do that, he helps the client to calm down and get very quiet. He says to the client, "In a moment I am going to say something to you. I'd like you to notice what happens in your body when I say it. Just notice what happens. And if nothing happens that's fine. We're just doing an experiment to help you learn some things about yourself."

Then Kurtz makes a nourishing statement to the client. For a client who is shrugging his or her shoulders, Kurtz may say, "You can trust yourself." For a client who is holding him or herself, he may say, "You are fine just the way you are." If Kurtz has correctly inferred what is going on beneath the surface, clients often have a visceral reaction to hearing such a nourishing statement. They don't believe it and that may trigger a rush of energy, numbness or queasiness in the stomach. That bodily sensation is a defense against the nourishing statement. Once the client notices the sensation and is following it, Kurtz may have an assistant "take over the defense" by placing a hand on the spot. Taking over the defense allows the client to let down the defense and let the emotion in. Often, clients go through a flood of emotion as they settle into the truth about what lies underneath the surface. Kurtz helps them use this experience to become aware of the hidden attitudes, beliefs and assumptions that are driving their behavior.[2] When I use this technique, I help clients get in touch with the bodily sensation and then ask them to tell me what the sensation would say to them if it had a voice. Typically, this helps them become aware of those unconscious dynamics that have been given various names by different therapists—deep structure, core material, schema.

There are other ways of helping clients become aware of these hidden forces. In chapter 1 I describe the "Connecting Bodily Sensations and Thoughts" exercise, a method which can help people to link their thoughts with their feelings and use that connection to become clearer about what they want to do to live more the way they want to live.

Clients can also be helped by learning from their dreams. Since dreams are the mind working when it is not under a person's conscious control, they can be windows to some of these unconscious dynamics.

Carl came to see me because he was experiencing severe psychosomatic symptoms. He spent much of his day in extreme pain or so tired he couldn't get out of bed. He was very hard on his wife and children and felt guilty about it. In one of our sessions he reported a dream in which he was the leader of a platoon that was engaged in a fierce battle. At one point, they made a miraculous escape from being trapped in a water-filled cistern, the walls of which were closing in on them. After the escape, as they rowed away in boats, Carl berated his men, brutally accusing them of being cowards, incompetents, weaklings. Through the dream, Carl became aware of how hard he was on himself, how he had set the bar so high for himself that it was impossible to meet it. As we worked together, he came to see just how damaging his perfectionism was to his wife, his children and himself. He learned that he was taking his shame and self-hatred out on them. He also began to see how his early experiences had affected him. Carl had been abandoned at a young age by his father and had tremendous pressure put on him to care for his mother and be the man of the house, even though he was a child. No matter how hard he tried, he wasn't able to live up to those expectations and suffered not only the shame, but also the lack of approval from his mother. Shortly after we worked on the dream, Carl had a "spontaneous" remission and gradually became free of the symptoms that had plagued him.

Sigmund Freud helped his clients get in touch with unconscious dynamics by having them lie on a couch and say everything that came to their minds. As they did so they were able to go deeper and deeper into their psyches and eventually begin to uncover some of that core material that was driving their behavior and creating problems and symptoms. As they became more comfortable on the couch they got below their defenses and they began to uncover thoughts, memories, beliefs and habits that were making life difficult for them.

One of the helpful things about the therapeutic process is that it aids clients in developing compassion for themselves. They become aware of how their early experiences have influenced their behavior. They understand that they didn't choose their parents but that their parents had a powerful impact on their behavior as adults.

Some people wonder about what good it does to dwell on the past or blame our problems on our parents. It is helpful, because it tells us that we weren't born this way. These habits, behaviors, traits and obsessions that plague us are the ways in which we learned to cope, survive, protect ourselves, feel more adequate and have the illusion of being okay. Since we weren't born with them but they grew in us as we did our best to survive, we have the power to overcome them and become healthier.

Once clients have become more accepting of and comfortable with what is true about themselves, are more clear about why they do what they do and don't do what they don't and have developed some compassion for themselves, the focus of therapy can turn to what the clients want and helping them move in that direction.

Here the therapist is helping clients get a better idea of the options that are available to them and helping choose among them. The therapist is also helping them gain some of the skills they will need to move forward—assertiveness, walking with fear, using anxiety and the stress response, managing their boundaries, using effective communication, making decisions, managing thoughts so they are helpful, not hurtful. The therapist also begins to confront the clients, to be the voice of reality.

At this point in therapy, clients often decide to do something to move in the direction in which they want to go. If they don't follow through, the topic of the next therapy session can be how they stopped themselves, what were they afraid of, what they wanted to have happen, what actually happened and what they can learn from that. This is the point at which therapists help clients to use their strengths, try out new behaviors and learn from what happens when they do.

This process will take at least six months and usually up to a year. If people are willing, able and ready to do this kind of intensive work, the payoff is huge. Clients become much more comfortable with themselves, can devote their energy to loving the way they want to love and expressing themselves the way they want instead of defending, hiding, repressing and getting in their own way. The clients learn how to manage themselves, their thoughts, feelings, intentions, perceptions, reactions and behavior. They learn how to get along with others without giving up too much of themselves. They develop a more balanced approach to life and learn how to use themselves effectively to get what they want. Since what they want is to love the way they want to love and express themselves the way they want to express themselves, other people are going to benefit.

Chapter 22

RECLAIMING THE BODY/ MIND'S SELF-HEALING POWERS

Scientific medicine has given us much for which to be thankful. It has greatly decreased the mortality rate from infectious diseases. It has wiped out polio. Through vaccines it has protected us against ailments that were once much more dangerous. We can transplant kidneys, lungs, livers and hearts. It is largely responsible for the steady increase in life expectancy that has occurred over the last forty years.

But there's a downside to scientific medicine: Our increasing reliance on it has led us to lose faith in the healing powers of the body/mind. Human beings have been evolving for millions of years. Over those eons we have developed a powerful natural capacity for self-healing. The human immune system is a marvel to behold. It is able to detect the presence of dangerous invaders—bacteria and viruses—and destroy them by secreting deadly chemicals, surrounding them and cutting them off from lifelines, inducing them to gorge themselves to death, etc. It also has the power to detect internal marauders—e.g., cancer cells—and kill them in various ways. Once it identifies a dangerous bacterium, virus or cancer cell, it remembers and is able to respond even more quickly and effectively to future invasions. It does this all by itself, without any conscious intervention by us. Of course, it can also turn on us and cause autoimmune diseases like Lupus and rheumatoid arthritis. When we're experiencing the stress response, it doesn't work very well. Still, it is a much more powerful tool for healing and protection than anything which scientific medicine has produced.

As we have discussed, all of the emotional and mental states we can experience have the potential to help us heal from traumas, fears, obsessions, feelings of inadequacy, loneliness and deep concerns about our lives. What we have come to call depression, bipolar disorder, anxiety disorders, psychosis and personality disorders are all potential paths toward healing and health.

The great weakness of scientific medicine is that it doesn't acknowledge the power of forces which can't as yet be measured, quantified and seen under microscopes, through laboratory tests or by other diagnostic instruments such as MRIs and PET scans. But some of those forces are powerful sources of healing. For example, we still don't know much about how the immune system works. We are especially in the dark about the connection between our minds and brains and the immune system. Candace Pert has identified neuropeptides that travel between the central nervous system and the immune system, carrying messages and controlling immune function.[1] But we know little about how they can be used to bolster the immune system. Scientific medicine has virtually no ability to strengthen or improve the functioning of the immune system.

Although we've learned a lot about how the brain and central nervous system function, what we don't know is much more important than what we do know. Although we know that people's brains change when they change the way in which they think and the way in which they process and use feelings, we don't know how that happens. We don't know the difference between what happens in the brain when we are planning a trip, making an important decision, just trying to understand something, concentrating on building or writing something or creating artwork. We don't even know what happens when we decide that we are going to move our arms in three seconds and then do it. Although some neuroscientists think they have a theory about how the brain creates the mind, they aren't even close to having a theory which meets the minimum requirements of legitimacy.

We know that love can heal, but we don't know how that works. We know there are spontaneous remissions from deadly cancers, but we don't know how that works. We know that humans who receive loving care, support, affirmation and nurturance from their parents—especially their mothers—early in life grow into healthier people than humans who don't, but we don't know much about how that works. The bottom line is that some of the most powerful forces for health and healing are not understood or even acknowledged by scientific medicine.

We have lost much of our understanding of and faith in the connection between the mind and the body. As we've seen, if a person is experiencing an intense stress response for a long period of time, his immune system will not be functioning very well and he is at serious risk of becoming ill. During the stress response, blood is going to the heart, brain and muscles and not to the digestive organs. No wonder that people under stress for long periods of time will develop liver, kidney, stomach and gall bladder problems.

My suggestion is that instead of putting all of our faith in scientific medicine, we allow ourselves to get back in touch with our powerful natural capacity for self-healing.

Chapter 23

TEN (PLUS THREE) TIPS TO HELP YOU ON YOUR WAY

1. Ask yourself what your "evil secrets" are. What are the parts of yourself that you don't like and try to hide from others? Now think of some of the ways you can use those parts of yourself to live more the way you want to live. Remember that your "evil secrets" are probably not very evil. They may be human and natural but not necessarily evil. We may have thought our negative emotions were evil because of messages we have gotten from our families, cultures, religions and teachers. But, using the information and exercises in this book, we have learned to travel within and take a more balanced and objective look at ourselves. And those "evil secrets" probably are not much of a secret either. Even though we've been spending lots of energy hiding them from other people, they've seen them in us. Like most things in the world, our evil secrets can be used for good or for ill depending on what we do with them. Finally, remember to honor your evil secrets when you are choosing a job, career or life path. If you use them well, they can be a big help.

2. The next time you feel angry, let it work inside you for about ten seconds. Then ask yourself what message you are getting from the anger. Listen to what your anger is telling you. What is it that you want to get rid of, protect yourself against

or overcome? How can you use the energy in your anger to do something about it? Remember that anger is a rush of energy. It is there because something is threatening you. There's something going on that you don't like, that you want to get rid of or protect yourself against. Anger is a very useful emotion, but what you do with it can be good or bad. It may also be useful to get in touch with any feelings that are underneath the anger. Often, lying just underneath is hurt, fear and shame. Sometimes, if you can connect with those feelings, you can learn something about yourself and let the anger go.

3. The next time you feel stressed—in your gut, your head, your chest, your eyes or anywhere else—ask yourself what is threatening you or what is being demanded of you. Stress is always a response to some threat or some demand. It may be something easy to deal with, like putting on your brakes to avoid hitting the car in front of you. But it may be something that is going to be very hard to deal with: a love relationship that is in trouble, a job that you hate and is getting the best of you, children who are going through hard times and need your help. In such cases, it's not going to be easy to deal with; if it were easy you would have already done it. Doing something about it is going to take some time, effort and courage. But if you don't do anything about it, the stress is going to linger and hurt you. The stress response is giving you the energy and the sharpness to deal with it. But you may decide that the timing isn't right, that you're going to have to live with this situation for a while. Whatever you decide, it is important to find ways of using the energy that is there. If you don't, it will eat you up inside. You can find several ways to do that by revisiting "Use the Energy in the Stress Response" in chapter 10. Anything that gets in the way of you loving the way you want to love, expressing yourself the way you want to express yourself (including work) or enjoying life the way you want to enjoy it will trigger the stress response.

4. Pay attention to what happens to you. Whenever something happens that you didn't want to have happen, ask yourself these questions:

   - How did I contribute to this happening?
   - Why might I have wanted this to happen?
   - What does this tell me about some of the underlying forces that are driving my behavior but of which I am not aware?

This is the most practical and accessible way of becoming aware of some of the underlying beliefs, attitudes, assumptions and habits that are driving your behavior. This is a very important step, because once you are aware of those underlying forces, you can manage them and keep them from getting in your way and creating problems.

The first question—How did I contribute to this happening?—is usually easy to answer, especially if you can be totally honest with yourself.

The second question—Why might I have wanted this to happen?—will take some more time and introspection. But it is a key step and is worth the time and effort. Previously, I told of a time when I sabotaged myself by giving a lousy speech to a convention when I had all of the knowledge and tools required to make a very good speech. The result was that, instead of proving myself a valuable member of the consulting team, I was fired. When I asked myself why I might have wanted that to happen, I became aware of the fact that I was afraid of becoming a powerful member of that team, because I didn't want that kind of pressure and expectations put on me. I also learned that I was very afraid of waging the kind of internal battles that have to be fought in a high-powered consulting firm out of fear that people wouldn't like me. I also learned that I didn't have much respect for the work this consulting firm did.

The final question—What does this tell me about some of the underlying forces that are driving my behavior but of which I am not aware?—is very similar to the second one. It assumes that when something happens to you that you didn't want to have happen and you contributed to it happening, there must be some underlying forces in you that had a part in it.

The bottom line of this step can be summed up in a dictum which was a centerpiece of a personal growth program that I attended: If you want to know what your intentions were, check the results.

5. Pay attention to the mistakes you make—mistakes of speaking, hearing, writing, forgetting, missing appointments, losing things, having accidents, etc. Ask yourself:

   - What is the meaning of this mistake?
   - What can this mistake tell me about what I want, what I don't want, what I'm afraid of, what I want to avoid, what I like, what I don't like?

   This is another practical way in which you can learn about what's going on underneath the surface of your consciousness. This is how Sigmund Freud learned of the power of unconscious dynamics over human behavior. He noticed that his clients made mistakes and that there was a pattern to the mistakes. They weren't random. They occurred in bunches or they were of a similar nature. From this he inferred that there was some meaning behind the mistakes. They were being driven by forces beneath the level of consciousness.

   As we discussed earlier, a good example of this unconscious drive is people who are always late. What are some of the possible drivers of their behavior? They want you to know that they are more important than you, their time is more valuable than yours, how busy they are. They want to make an entrance or they just don't want to be there. But this isn't accidental or random behavior. Something beneath the surface is driving it.

6. The next time you're aware of feeling bad, down, sad, depressed, anxious and/or stressed, ask yourself these questions:

- What am I thinking? What thoughts are in my head? Are these automatic negative thoughts?
- To what extent are these thoughts realistic, supported by evidence and helpful?
- What are some other thoughts I could have that are more realistic and helpful?
- If the thoughts that are in my head are negative, not realistic or useful, where are they coming from? What is behind them? What do they do for me?
- What in my life has led me to have this pattern of negative thoughts?

Perhaps we are using these negative thoughts to keep ourselves safe, to avoid taking risks and to avoid putting pressure on ourselves. Are we using these thoughts to stop ourselves from getting what we want? What would be scary about getting what we want?

7. The next time you find yourself feeling jealous, ask yourself:

- Where is this jealousy coming from?
- What is it telling me about what I want and don't have?
- What can I do to get that?
- Why do I want it?

As we have seen, knowing what you want is very important. Getting in touch with your jealousy can tell you what you want and don't have.

8. The next time you find yourself afraid, ask yourself:

- What am I afraid of exactly?
- What is the worst thing that can happen?

Use your intuition to decide if you are going to walk with the fear or stay away from what you are afraid of and protect yourself.

Fear is a hard emotion to manage. Knowing the difference between the fear you should walk with and the fear you should pay attention to is a challenge. Irrational and excessive fear is one of the ways we stop ourselves from getting what we want. Once you've answered the reflective questions, your best option is to trust that you know whether to walk with the fear or pay attention to it.

9. Work at learning from your dreams. If you don't remember your dreams, put a pad and pencil or pen by your bed and, as soon as you are barely awake, write down your dream. You may recall only brief snatches or a few disjointed images. Write them down. Even fragments of dreams can be useful. Before you go to sleep, tell yourself that you want to remember your dream so you can learn from it. Once you remember even a small part of your dream, use some way of listening to the message from it, learning what it has to tell you. One method of doing this is by reviewing "Learning From Your Dreams" in chapter 12.

10. The next time you experience the symptoms of a panic attack—heart palpitations, shortness of breath, sweating, numbness in your fingers and toes, dizziness and faintness, a feeling like you're having a heart attack or stroke—focus on something outside of yourself and tell yourself: *I know what this is. This is a panic attack. I've gotten through these before. I'll get through this one.*

When it's over, ask yourself:

- Am I facing some problem that is so difficult it doesn't have any good solution, so difficult that I don't even want to know what it is?

- Is there a dilemma that I am facing that is so difficult that it doesn't have a good outcome but does have a less worse one?

This is very hard to do, but it is worth making a real effort, because it can have a big payoff. I have had panic attacks at various times in my life and, at the time, didn't know what the causes were. Now when I look back, I know exactly what they were a result of. Had I been able to become aware of the dilemmas I was facing, I may have been able to deal with the attacks in a better way.

11. Take your sex life seriously. If you don't have a partner, take action to find one. If you still don't have a partner, find some wonderful, creative, exciting ways of masturbating. If you have a partner but sex has dwindled, get some help. In most medium-sized and larger communities there are trained sex therapists who can help couples build satisfying sex lives.

Even though sex is played up on television, in movies and magazines and on the Internet, I don't think we take it seriously enough. We think that we can do without it, that it's not that big a deal. But it is a big deal. In one study of men who had suffered heart attacks, it turned out that more than half of them had not had sex in the year previous to the heart attack. The conclusion was that perhaps regular and satisfying sex could "inoculate" against heart attacks.

12. The next time you are aware that you are facing a dilemma, a problem that doesn't seem to have any good answer but, perhaps, has some less worse ones, see if you can use your imagination to honor both sides of the dilemma and come up with a resolution that you feel is the best you can do— even if it isn't so good.

One thing that you can do to help yourself is to set up a couple of chairs facing each other and have a conversation between the parts of yourself that are on opposite sides of the conflict. Let's say the dilemma you are facing has to do with your job. You've been in the job for five years. You're tired of it; it has lost its challenge. You're ready to move on to something else. But the timing isn't right. You have young children. Your wife is a stay-at-home mom. Still, you are very frustrated at work and the stress is getting to you. Set up the chairs and have a conversation between the part of yourself that wants to change jobs and the part that wants to remain at the one you have. You change chairs as if the two parts of yourself are talking to each other. This helps, because you are getting the internal dialogue out of your head, you can hear your voice and the energy in it and you can get a better idea about the real issue and where you stand on it. In the process of the conversation you may come up with some options you hadn't thought of. It's not necessary to make a quick decision on the basis of this conversation. You can leave the issue for a while, let the conversation work in your mind and, hopefully, find a good way to resolve the dilemma.

13. The next time you are aware that somebody is behaving in a way that is a problem for you, bring it up with him or her in a way that won't harm your relationship, make the person defensive or make things worse. Here are some hints about how to do this:

- When you bring up the problem, simply describe what you have noticed. Don't evaluate it. Just describe it. Let's suppose that one of your colleagues in the medical clinic where you work has stopped referring clients to you. You approach the person and say, "I notice that you haven't been referring as many clients to me as you had in the past."

- Describe how this is a problem for you. You might say something like, "I'm having a problem with it, because

I like to work with clients and I don't know what has happened to change things." Invite the other person to work with you on addressing the problem.

- Be direct rather than strategic or manipulative. You don't want to say something such as, "How would you like it if I stopped referring clients to you?" or "What's going on, anyway?"

- Be understanding. You might let the person know that you realize he or she has other things to worry about besides making referrals to you.

- Be provisional, not certain. Let the person know you don't have an answer to the problem but you'd like to work on it with him or her.

Afterword

THE SERENDIPITY OF IT ALL

I have given you some ideas, approaches and exercises to help you use your dark side—the parts of yourself that are scary, dangerous, painful, shameful and hidden—to build a satisfying life. Some people see the dark side as being associated with the Devil, with evil. I see it as a part of yourself that is natural, in tune with nature and the natural world, more like other animals.

We have discussed how you can:

- Use the so-called "negative" emotions of anger, fear, jealousy, anxiety, sadness and guilt to become more clear about what is important and precious, what you want, what you don't want and what you want to get rid of and keep out of your life.

- Use the stress response to know what is threatening your ability to love and work the way you want to and to do something about it.

- Learn valuable lessons about yourself through exploring your automatic negative thinking and learn how to manage your thoughts so they are helpful, not harmful.

- Become aware of some of the beliefs, assumptions, feelings and attitudes that lie deep below your consciousness so that you can manage them for your benefit.

- Get along with important others in your life without giving up too much of yourself.

- Manage your boundary so that the behavior of others and their reactions to you don't keep you from living the way you want to live.

- Become more friendly with the parts of yourself you don't like and wish weren't there and instead use them for your benefit.

- Become more serious about your sex life and do what you can to make it more satisfying and health-enhancing.

- Use your "symptoms" as a way of learning more about yourself and becoming more skilled at managing your thoughts, feelings, intentions and behavior.

If you build a satisfying life you'll be psychologically healthy. If you are psychologically healthy, you will also be physically healthy. In fact, the dichotomy between psychological health and physical health is a false one. Psychology and biology are inextricably intertwined. All psychological variables are biological and are expressed biologically. And all biological phenomena are affected by and are essentially manifestations of psychological variables. I have used the term "body/mind" as a reflection of this truth.

I am aware that some people may look upon those of us who spend a lot of time working on ourselves and building and maintaining our health as selfish and self-centered. But, as I noted previously, there is a wonderful synergy at work here. Since the key to being healthy lies in finding ways to express our natural drives to love and work in ways that are satisfying to us, as we become more able to do that, as we build our capacities to love and work as we want to, others will benefit: our spouses, parents, children, friends, customers, colleagues, our fellow humans. How fortunate. We can harness our negative emotions, our dark sides, to build better lives for ourselves and those who are close to us. We can build a better world.

Acknowledgements

I suppose you could say that the germination of this book began when I first realized that I was separate from other people and that I had some control over what I thought and how I behaved. That would have occurred somewhere around age three. That would mean that I am indebted to all of the people who have helped me learn how to manage my thoughts, feelings, intentions and behavior, to pick up the pieces when I haven't been able to do that well enough to avoid getting into trouble and to hang in there with me when I was being a jerk.

So without naming names (you know who you are), here is a partial list:

My wife.
My children.
My parents.
My nanny.
My siblings.
My in-laws.
My friends at Castle Village in upper Manhattan.
My teachers at P.S. 187 in Manhattan.
The wonderful friends of my parents.
My friends at Valley Cottage Elementary School and
    Nyack High School.
My coaches and teachers there.

My brothers at Alpha Phi Delta fraternity at Cornell University.

Other friends at Cornell.

My fellow Peace Corps volunteers and the staff of the Peace Corps Training Center in Puerto Rico.

All of my therapists.

All of my patients.

All of my psychologist supervisors.

My friends and teachers at the Fels Institute for Local and State Government Administration.

My colleagues at the City of Albuquerque, the Southern Rio Grande Council of Governments, the City of Las Cruces, The Institute for Gerontological Research and Education at New Mexico State University, McManis Associates and the Las Cruces Public Schools.

My great friends in Las Cruces.

My tennis, basketball, baseball, softball and golf playing buddies.

My colleagues and clients at Niagara Mohawk Power Corporation.

My mentors at Onondaga Pastoral Counseling Center in Syracuse and the Massachusetts Society for the Prevention of Cruelty to Children (MSPCC) in Holyoke, MA.

My fellow therapists at MSPCC.

The members of my Doctoral Committee at The Union Institute.

My fellow learners at The Union Institute.

My colleagues at The Salud Family Health Centers in Fort Lupton, CO.

All of the editors, readers and supporters who have helped me with this book.

The authors of the books that have been so helpful to me.

I am particularly indebted to these authors and their works:

Antonio Damasio and his book *Descartes' Error.*
M. Scott Peck and his book *People of the Lie.*
Thomas Moore and his book *Care of the Soul.*
Eugene Gendlin and his book *Focusing.*
Robert Sapolsky and his study of baboons.
Hans Selye and his work on stress and the stress response.
Friedrich Perls and his work on gestalt therapy.
Aaron Beck and his work on cognitive therapy.
Albert Ellis and his work on rational emotive therapy.
Sigmund and Ana Freud and their work on unconscious
    dynamics and defense mechanisms.
Robert Johnson and his book *Inner Work.*
David Schnarch and his book *Passionate Marriage.*
George Bach and his book *The Intimate Enemy.*
Harville Hendrix and his book *Getting the Love You Want.*
Jack Gibb and his work on non-defensive communication.
Thomas Gordon and his work on active listening.
Pat Ogden and her work on boundary management and
    trauma therapy.
David Maister and his work on the use of evil secrets.
Carl Jung and his work on integrating the shadow.
Jon Kabat-Zinn and his work on mindfulness meditation.

There are two people who deserve special mention. One is my wife, Nancy Fletcher Galves, who has been a constant source of support and affirmation and who, thankfully, has been willing to engage with me in the battles that are necessary to growing up and becoming whole. The other is Dr. Richard L. Hopkins who, through a remarkable display of courage, wisdom and compassion, provided me with crucial support at the darkest time of my life and who has been my friend, confidante and fellow traveler ever since.

Notes

Prologue

1. "Phineas Gage," Wikipedia, http://en.wikipedia.org/wiki/Phineas_Gage.
2. Antonio Damasio, *Descartes' Error* (New York: G.P. Putnam, 1994).

Chapter 2

1. Nico H. Frijda, "The laws of emotion," *American Psychologist* 43, no. 5 (May 1988): 349–358.
2. J.W. Pennebaker and R. Kiecolt-Glaser, "Disclosure of trauma and immune function: Health implications for psychotherapy," *Journal of Consulting and Clinical Psychology* 56 (1990): 239–245.
3. Nicholas R. S. Hall, Maureen O'Grady and Denis Calandra, "Transformation of personality and the immune system," *Advances* 10, no. 4 (Fall 1994): 7–15.
4. *Brain-Mind Bulletin* 12, no. 2 (1987): 2.
5. A.O. Galves, "An Experiment in Psychological Wellness" (Doctoral Dissertation, The Union Institute, 1997).

Chapter 3

1. Alice Miller, "The drama of the gifted child and the psychoanalyst's narcissistic disturbance," *International Journal of Psychoanalysis* 60 (1979): 47–58.

Chapter 5

1. E.J. Teng et al., "When anxiety symptoms masquerade as medical symptoms: What medical specialists know about panic disorder and available psychological treatments," *Journal of Clinical Psychology in Medical Settings* 15, no. 4 (2008): 314–321.
2. M. Zeidner, "Test anxiety and aptitude test performance in actual college admission testing situation," *Personality and Individual Differences* 12, no. 2 (1991): 101–109.

3. Rollo May, *The Meaning of Anxiety* (New York: W.W. Norton & Company, Inc., 1977), 363.

4. May, *The Meaning of Anxiety*; Søren Kierkegaard, *The Concept of Dread*, trans. Walter Lowrie (Princeton, NJ: Princeton University Press, 1944).

Chapter 6

1. Ayala Malach Pines, *Romantic Jealousy: Causes, Symptoms, Cures* (New York: Routledge, 1998), quoted in David Buss, *The Dangerous Passion: Why Jealousy Is as Necessary as Love and Sex* (New York: The Free Press, 2000).

2. David Buss, *The Dangerous Passion: Why Jealousy is as Necessary as Love and Sex* (New York: The Free Press, 2000).

3. Ibid.

4. Ibid.

Chapter 7

1. F. V. DeGruy, "Mental healthcare in the primary care setting: A paradigm problem," *Families, Systems and Health* 15, no.1 (1997): 3–26.

Chapter 9

1. Damasio, *Descartes' Error.*

2. Peter Kramer, *Listening to Prozac* (New York: Viking, 1993).

Chapter 10

1. Hans Selye, *Stress Without Distress* (Philadelphia: J.P. Lippincott, 1974).

2. Ibid.

3. Robert Sapolsky, S.C. Alberts and J. Altmann, "Hypercortisolism associated with social subordination or social isolation among wild baboons," *Archives of General Psychiatry* 54, no. 12 (1997): 1137–1143.

4. T. Farley, A. Galves, M. Garcia and P. Wilkinson, "Stress, coping and health: A comparison of Mexican immigrants, Mexican-Americans and Non-Hispanic Whites," *Journal of Immigrant Health* 7, no. 3 (2005).

5. F.S. Perls, *Gestalt Therapy Verbatim*, ed. John O. Stevens (Lafayette, CA: Real People Press, 1969).

6. Ibid.

Chapter 11

1. Paul Watson, N. Mitchell and E. Hagen, "The evolution of depression: Does it have a role?" *All in the Mind*, April 3, 2004, http://www.abc.net .au/rn/allinthemind/stories/2004/1077027.htm.
2. Albert Ellis, *Reason and Emotion in Psychotherapy* (Seaucus, NJ: Lyle Stuart, 1975).
3. Ibid.
4. Aaron Beck, *Cognitive Therapy and the Emotional Disorders* (New York: International Universities Press, 1976).

Chapter 12

1. Robert Johnson, *Inner Work: Using Dreams and Active Imagination for Personal Growth* (New York: HarperCollins, 1986).
2. George E. Vaillant, *Adaptation to Life* (Cambridge, MA: Harvard University Press, 1998).

Chapter 13

1. Jack Gibb, "Non-defensive communication," *The Journal of Communication* 11, no. 3 (September 1961): 141–148.
2. Thomas Gordon, *Parent Effectiveness Training: The Proven Program for Raising Responsible Children* (New York: Three Rivers Press, 2000).
3. Thomas Moore, *Care of the Soul: A Guide for Cultivating Depth and Sacredness in Everyday Life* (New York: HarperCollins, 1992).
4. C. Wedekind et al., "MHC-dependent mate preferences in humans," *Proceedings of the Royal Society of London Series B* 260 (1995): 245–249.
5. David Schnarch, *Passionate Marriage: Love, Sex, and Intimacy in Emotionally Committed Relationships* (New York: W.W. Norton & Company, 1997).
6. Pat Ogden, *Exploring Boundaries* (Hakomi Integrative Somatics, 2001).

Chapter 14

1. Perls, *Gestalt Therapy Verbatim*.
2. Moore, *Care of the Soul.*

Chapter 15

1. J.E Muller et al., "Triggering myocardial infarction by sexual activity: Low absolute risk and prevention by regular physical exercise," *Journal of the American Medical Association* 275 (1996): 1405–1409.
2. Ibid. *Journal of the American Medical Association* 275 (1996): 1405–1409.

Chapter 16

1. *Diagnostic and Statistical Manual of Mental Disorders,* 4th ed., text rev. (Washington, DC: America Psychiatric Association, 2000).
2. Watson, Mitchell and Hagen, "The evolution of depression."
3. Ibid.
4. Moore, *Care of the Soul.*
5. Damasio, *Descartes' Error.*
6. Harvey Jackins, *The Human Side of Human Beings: The Theory of Re-Evaluation Counseling* (Seattle: Rational Island Publishers, 1978).
7. M. Babyak et al., "Exercise treatment for major depression: Maintenance of therapeutic benefit at 10 months," *Psychosomatic Medicine* 62, no. 5 (2000): 633–638.

Chapter 17

1. *Diagnostic and Statistical Manual of Mental Disorders.*
2. J. Becker, *Affective Disorders* (Morristown, NJ: General Learning Press, 1977).
3. Kay Redfield Jamison, *An Unquiet Mind* (New York: Vintage, 1997).
4. M.B. Cohen et al., "An intensive study of twelve cases of manic-depressive psychosis," *Psychiatry: Journal for the Study of Interpersonal Processes* 17 (1954): 103–137.
5. J Blechert, "Hypomanic personality is a predictor of bipolar disorder," *British Journal of Clinical Psychology* 44 no.1 (2005): 15-27.
6. Sean Blackwell, "Beyond Meds," www.bipolarblast.wordpress.com (accessed on June 15, 2009).

Chapter 18

1. *Merriam-Webster's Collegiate Dictionary,* 10th ed., s.v. "anxiety."
2. Selye, *Stress Without Distress.*

3. Teng et al., "When anxiety symptoms masquerade as medical symptoms."
4. *Diagnostic and Statistical Manual of Mental Disorders.*
5. Jeffrey Schwartz et al., "Systematic changes in cerebral glucose metabolic rate after successful behavior modification treatment of obsessive compulsive disorder," *Archives of General Psychiatry* 53, no. 2 (1996): 109–113.
6. *Diagnostic and Statistical Manual of Mental Disorders.*
7. James Pennebaker and R. Kiecolt-Glaser, "Disclosure of trauma and immune function: Health implications for psychotherapy," *Journal of Consulting and Clinical Psychology* 56 (1990): 239–245.

Chapter 19

1. John Weir Perry, *The Far Side of Madness* (Englewood Cliffs, NJ: Prentice Hall, 1974).
2. Miller, "The drama of the gifted child."
3. Julius Lanoil, interview with author.
4. J. Bola et al., "Treatment of acute psychosis without neuroleptics. Two-year outcomes from the Soteria project," *Journal of Nervous Mental Disease* 191 (2003): 219–229.

Chapter 20

1. Moore, *Care of the Soul.*

Chapter 21

1. Perls, *Gestalt Therapy Verbatim.*
2. R. Kurtz, *Body-Centered Psychotherapy: The Hakomi Method* (Mendocino, CA: LifeRhythm, 1990).

Chapter 22

1. Candace Pert, *Molecules in Motion: Why You Feel the Way You Feel* (New York: Touchstone, 1999).